Cat Conundrums

Pet Peeves

Cat Conundrums

Simple Solutions to Everyday Problems

GARY R. SAMPSON, DVM, with DICK WOLFSIE

Copyright© 2005 by Gary R. Sampson and Dick Wolfsie
All rights reserved. No portion of this book may be reproduced in any fashion, print, facsimile, or electronic, or by any method yet to be developed, without express permission of the copyright holder.

For further information, contact the publisher at

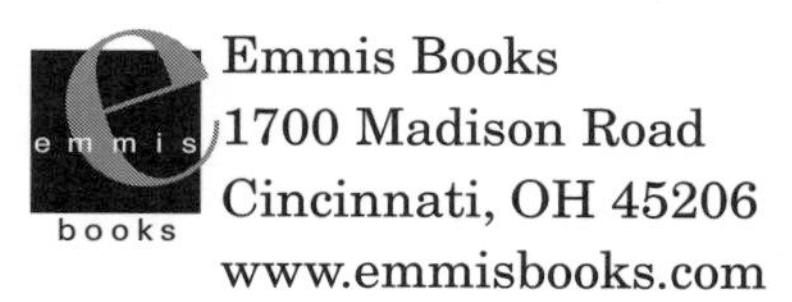

Emmis Books
1700 Madison Road
Cincinnati, OH 45206
www.emmisbooks.com

Library of Congress Cataloging-in-Publication Data

Sampson, Gary R.
Cat conundrums : simple solutions to everyday problems / Gary R. Sampson with Dick Wolfsie.
p. cm. -- (Pet peeves)
ISBN 1-57860-227-0 (pbk.)
1. Cats--Behavior. I. Wolfsie, Dick. II. Title. III. Series.
SF446.5.S26 2005
636.8'088'7--dc22

2005001352

Designed by Andrea Kupper
Edited by Jessica Yerega

DEDICATION

I dedicate this book to all the veterinarians who have shared their practices with me by referring clients and patients, thus keeping me challenged and deepening my knowledge of cats.

And to my beloved pet Elaine, my wife of forty-seven years, who encouraged me to share my stories.

And, finally, to all my cats over the years—Mitzi, Timmy and Tammy, Sasha and Sam. Thank you. You all taught me so much.

Contents

Part Three: Anxiety

Part Four: Destruction

Part Five: Other Misbehaviors

Introduction

As a veterinarian who limits his practice to dog and cat behavior modification, I have been dealing with the misbehavior of humans for twenty years.

Of course, humans are not completely responsible for the conduct of their pets. All animal behavior is a curious combination of the animal's instincts and the effects of the conditions he is raised in. But, yes, *you* are the conditions.

The relationship between man and cat goes back tens of thousands of years. And both parties are pretty happy with the arrangement. Humans acquired an animal capable of reciprocal affection, not just a lap warmer and companion but a portable rodent controller. Cats got a pretty good deal, as well. It's a lot easier to wait for your food to be put in a bowl than foraging for survival. And I kind of think that getting rubbed on the cheeks was the cat's idea.

Over time, the cat became more and more domesticated, gradually moving from the barn, to the porch, to the kitchen, and finally into the bedroom. The feline's distinctive personality became part of the family dynamics. Now, when I hear about cats that sleep under the covers, I wonder if things haven't gone too far.

In fact, this is probably the reason you have purchased this book. You have a cat that does not fit your image of how a family pet should behave. Your kitten has destroyed your couch; your six-year-old Persian will not use the litter box. The family cat has started to nip and bite for the first time. These are pretty common problems, but, as you will discover, every cat is different. Every owner is different. Every situation is different.

My role is to help you understand why your cat prefers your suitcase to the litter box, or why your kitty would rather sleep on your husband's lap than yours—and your husband hates cats. If there were simple solutions to these problems, I would just fax my clients a checklist of dos and don'ts. But it doesn't work that way.

In our first phone conversation I want the owner to tell me all about the cat. Among other things, I inquire about the cat's background and how he fits into the family. Of course, I want to know exactly what the problem is and how it has been dealt with up to this point.

I am not content with just offering a solution. I want my clients to understand how the problem developed, because it gives them a better appreciation of how my directions for addressing the issue have a pretty good chance of working.

My suggestions are successful only when the client is willing and able to make a commitment to change his or her behavior. Because only then will the cat's behavior change. That's not always easy. For example, in some cases, I may tell a client *not* to let their cat see outside cats. "That's the worst thing you can do," I'll say. That seems odd to some people, but that's where a full explanation is so important. Then when the client says, "Oh, *now* I see why you said that," that's a pretty good indication my advice has been heard and understood and may be taken.

Every day in this country, thousands of people abandon their cats or relinquish them to humane societies and animal shelters. Why? Because their cat has a behavior problem that they cannot deal with. And sadly, it is probably a behavior problem they contributed to or are inadvertently reinforcing. That's where I come in. The people who call me love their pets and are looking for assistance. But for the thousands of people each year who might give up on their cats, I hope this book will be a wake-up call that help is available.

All the stories are based on real cases, though on occasion I have combined incidents so that a more typical example can be represented. You'll meet a cat who stood guard over his litter box and one that played hockey with his feces—just a parade of quirky behaviors that stumped my clients but will both amuse and educate you about your pet.

By the way, if your cat loves to scratch, make sure she can't reach this book. And don't miss the chapter titled "Living Out a Scratching." Now there was a cat that could sink its claws into a good book.

Barney, Dick Wolfsie, and Me

Although I have worked with thousands of dog and cat owners, I am probably best known for the six minutes I spent on a TV show with Dick Wolfsie in the fall of 1992. That episode is chronicled in Dick's book about his infamous dog. People ask me about it even now, years later.

Dick found Barney on his front step in 1991, and it wasn't long before the renegade little pooch was eating, chewing, and digging himself into deep trouble. Because Dick's wife could not tolerate the dog's destructiveness, she "encouraged" Dick to take Barney with him to work each morning during his show on WISH-TV.

At that time, I was beginning a new chapter in my life, as well. For thirty years I had been employed as an industrial veterinarian working to develop animal health products. But beginning in the mid-1980s, I decided to develop a veterinary practice limited to dog and cat behavior problems—always an interest of mine.

I had been watching Dick Wolfsie on TV for several years and, like so many viewers, was captivated by his new TV companion. For me, their relationship was especially endearing because as a young boy, I, too, had a beagle. His name was Duffy.

Now Duffy was not my first pet. The honor goes to Mitzi, a kitten I brought home from my cousin's farm to the great surprise of my parent's. Even as a nine-year-old boy, I was fascinated with her behavior. Maybe that's how it all started.

Gary Sampson and Mitzi, circa 1945.

But back to beagles, a spirited, inquisitive, high-energy breed that will love you to death, but also be the death of you. They are diggers, chewers, chow hounds, and escape artists. That's how I remembered Duffy. Duffy was also the neighborhood stud. In fact, I used Duffy the "love machine" as a way to make money to purchase my first car, renting out Duffy's services to people who wanted to breed beagles.

Gary Sampson and Duffy, circa 1950.

Duffy also did occasional freelance work, sometimes gone days at a time. My mother kept a calendar of which dogs in the neighborhood were in heat, so if Duffy missed a meal (which beagles seldom do) she'd have a pretty good idea of what had detained him and where I should go to get him.

At the suggestion of Dick's veterinarian, he called me in search of some answers on how to stop Barney's incessant digging and chewing.

Despite my normally reticent demeanor, Dick somehow convinced me to come on live television and discuss the problems he was having with Barney. To this day, I don't know why I agreed to this, but I am sure that fond memories of Duffy played a big role. The fact that I might get a little publicity for my fledgling practice was also a factor. But this was live television! I sure didn't want to put my paw in my mouth.

The morning of the show, I arrived at Dick's, where the foreboding TV remote truck sat in front of his house. I soon learned that the show was almost cancelled because Barney had dug under the fence the night before and had been found only in the past hour or so, several miles from Dick's home. Shades of Duffy again. This was not going to be an easy case.

Dick did everything he could to make me feel comfortable, like going over all the questions he was going to ask me. That made me feel better at first, but when the live interview started, his first question came out of left field. I stammered, collecting my thoughts for a moment, and then I felt some dirt hit me in the face. Then a splat on my shirt. And my shoes. Dick was equally targeted.

Dick and I looked over as the TV camera panned, and we watched in amazement while Barney began excavating a rose bush right in front of us. The dirt and mud were flying, and what followed was not an interview but two full minutes of us laughing. I attempted a few token observations about why dogs like to dig, but if I did make any good points, they were literally buried as the dog's behavior took center stage.

After the commercial break, we decided we'd switch gears and talk about Barney's chewing problem. Dick went into his house and got an array of items that Barney had virtually destroyed in the previous week—items ranging from balls and Frisbees to TV remote controls to his wife's brand new high-heeled shoes and his son's stuffed animals. They weren't stuffed anymore.

As the break ended, I noticed that the cameraman seemed befuddled about something. He was waggling the wires and checking connections. "I have no audio," I heard him tell Dick. This struck us all as odd. The previous segment had been free of any technical problems.

Sad to say, we never did do that next segment. We never did discuss why Barney loved to chew. We couldn't. Barney had chewed the microphone cord in half.

That is my memory of how I first met Dick Wolfsie. I lost touch with Dick for many years, but when Barney died I dropped him a note. Again, Barney's death had rekindled thoughts of Duffy. Dick followed up with a phone call, and as we reminisced about our first meeting, the idea of this book was born. I knew I had many humorous case studies and helpful advice to share from my twenty years of treating behavior problems in dogs and cats, and I knew that Dick had a knack for telling stories in a fun and informative way.

By the way, Duffy lived to a ripe old age. At the age of twenty, I married Elaine (my wife of forty-seven years). The beagle remained with my parents. It was my turn to leave home for a little romance of my own.

A final note. Dick Wolfsie has a new beagle named Toby. He also has a twenty-year-old cat named Benson. Apparently, the two have not been getting along, and Dick asked me to go on TV with him again and discuss how to make the duo more compatible.

I told Dick I would be glad to help. But I don't think this will make very good television. Unless you like watching two people talk on the phone.

CAT NIPS

- Spay/neuter your dog and cat. You want to be a responsible owner, not the godfather of the entire neighborhood canine and feline population.

- There are indoor cats, outdoor cats, and indoor/outdoor cats. Given a choice, I'd have indoor cats.

Part One

Litter Box/ Elimination Problems

"Cats don't like change without their consent."

—Roger A. Caras

"Dogs come when they're called; cats take a message and get back to you later."

—Mary Bly

Chapter 1

THE CAT SCANNER

Domino the cat had a great job. He sat on top of the litter box most of the day and terrorized Vinegar and Olive Oyl, the other two cats in the family. When Vinegar and Olive Oyl tried to get in the box, Domino hissed and swatted at them. If they did manage to get in the box when he did not see them, he'd often ambush them when they exited, scaring them half to death.

Okay, it wasn't a great job. It didn't pay anything. It was volunteer stuff. But the work was steady. Very steady. And Domino was a great employee. He never missed a day. Or night.

Needless to say, this created a lot of stress with V. and O., who began to realize that the fastidious litter box thing was not the pleasant experience their instincts had directed them to. When they did manage to get in the box, they hurried out in fear. Then Domino would go inside and do the paper work: burying the urine or feces himself. His attitude was: If you want a job done right, do it yourself.

Edith $apper was the lady of the house. That's no misprint in her name. Mrs. $apper lived on Chicago's Michigan Avenue in a small but expensive condo overlooking the lake. She had plenty of money, but she'd have given up half her fortune to have a little harmony in the family. When Vinegar and Olive Oyl completely abandoned their traditional restrooms because of Domino, they found new and safer places to go—including a seven-thousand-dollar Persian rug. That's when Mrs. $ sought professional help.

We both recognized that three cats in a tiny apartment was not the best situation. Cats are territorial, and forcing a close proximity was a recipe for problems. Plus, Domino was a male cat, and it is not unusual for the man of the house to feel in control. In fact, his control of the litter box was exactly that: a show of dominance.

First, I expressed my personal preference for boxes without a top. Initially, this would discourage Domino from assuming his sentinel position, although, as you will learn, Domino was a pretty ingenious feline.

I told Mrs. $apper to increase the number of litter boxes and spread them out in the bedroom, living room, and kitchen so that V. and O. always had a choice and the terrorizing could be minimized. But the problem was that the condo was relatively small, and no matter where she placed the boxes, Domino situated himself in such a position that he could still monitor them pretty well. With four boxes to watch, however, he was probably getting a major headache.

We then tried separating him from Vinegar and Olive Oyl by confining him to the bedroom during the day while Mrs. $apper was at work. This eliminated some of the stress in the house so that V. and O. could have some pee and quiet. I also suggested that Mrs. $ alternate which cats could spend the night in her bedroom, but let them be together when she was home during the day and could monitor them. I even encouraged that she put a bell on Domino's collar so that the other cats could keep track of where Domino was. We didn't want to isolate them altogether, because ultimately we did want them all to live happily under one roof.

All things considered, we were pretty successful—all urine and feces were back in the boxes. Domino must have been on overload trying to watch four litter boxes and decided to cut back on his hours. But still, Mrs $ sensed that harmony had not been fully established, which was really her overriding concern. It was then that she called for one last conversation.

"Dr. Sampson, I just want you to know that my three cats are the most expensive pets in Chicago."

"My fees are very reasonable, I assure you."

"No, it's not your fee. I decided to move so my cats would have more space and get along. I bought a bigger condo. It just cost me another half million."

She was right. Mrs. $ had the most expensive cats in Chicago.

CAT NIPS

- Litter boxes with tops usually please only the owner, not the cat. The top holds in odors and makes it hard to determine when the box is dirty, so the cat will know it's dirty before you do.

- On the other hand, some cats like total privacy in the box. If you think you have a cat like that, the top may be necessary.

- Male cats often dominate and control females. Thinking of a second cat? You have a better chance of harmony if both cats are the same gender.

Chapter 2

FINE FOR LITTERING

Cat owners rejoice that cats, unlike dogs, usually require no special training to learn how to deposit their waste in the proper place. It's instinctive and reinforced by their mothers. Housebreaking a dog, despite what every book says, can be troublesome at times—and it takes a little work on the part of both the pooch and the owner. For cat owners it's a slam dunk.

Usually!

Surprisingly, I have received dozens of calls over the years from frustrated cat owners who claim that their cat seems to have missed the boat when it came to acquiring this instinctive behavior. Or, in some cases, the cat has the instinct, but what he is missing is the box.

When Edgar and Twila Crookshanks called me one morning about their cat, Ching, I listened carefully as the elderly couple took turns on the phone expressing concern about their cat's apparent disregard for what should have been basic instinctual behavior: Deposit waste in the sand; cover it up; catch mice.

Instead, Ching was leaving his waste alongside the box. Usually when cats avoid their litter box, they *really* avoid it, often opting for a corner in a another room. But these deposits had just barely missed the receptacle.

I went through my normal litany of questions about the cleanliness of the box, explaining that some cats are so fastidious that they will not eliminate in a box that is soiled at all. In fact, most cats want to urinate and defecate in different receptacles. I told the Crookshanks that the rule of thumb for boxes is to have at least two boxes for one cat and three or four boxes for two cats. And as cats age, they become even more meticulous about their boxes. Just like humans, when cats get older, they get a bit more finicky.

After following my advice, another call made it clear that none of this seemed to address the problem. I was assured that the boxes were kept scrupulously clean, so I suspected that the problem might be the litter itself. I recommended that they "slope" the kitty litter in the box (three inches on one end, sloped to a quarter-inch for the last third of the box) affording the cat firm ground on one end of the box to get his footing. Many cats are spooked by the shifting "sands" of kitty litter, which is why many cats will prefer your carpeting with its solid base.

After these further changes it was obvious that this was not the problem, either. At that point, I suspected that their dog Pepi, a toy poodle, might be the source of the enigma. Dogs are attracted to the kitty litter box because the feline waste is considered a delicacy by canine gourmets. It smells good, it tastes good, and you can eat it fresh out of the box.

As a result, some dogs will practically stalk the family cat, waiting for him to leave a treat behind. Cats, who already prefer privacy in these matters, may opt to find another location for their daily squat rather than contend with a dog whose motto is: Waste makes taste.

Again, my thoughts did not seem pertinent to this case. But after the third phone call, I sensed there was something that I wasn't being told or had failed to understand. I often get that feeling. Information is seldom withheld on purpose by a client; instead, data goes undisclosed because the client doesn't think the behavior in question is relevant. Of course, I could blame myself for not soliciting the necessary facts, but I'll let you decide.

During this phone call I was once again desperately seeking a clue to this mystery, when Mrs. Crookshank, who was on the extension phone, casually said to her hubby:

"Edgar, did you ever tell Dr. Sampson about Pepi's weird behavior?"

"Oh, sweetheart, don't be silly. What could this possibly have to do with the problem?"

I was beginning to see some light at the end of the puzzle. Animal and human behavior in a family are often connected. If they had a dog that was doing something a bit odd, it could clearly have something to do with the cat's eccentric conduct.

"What is Pepi doing?" I asked, and held my breath. I could almost see it coming.

Mr. Crooskshank explained that, ever since his knee surgery, he hadn't been able to walk Pepi as often, a change of events that altered the normal constitutional activities of his dog. To compensate, Pepi had begun using the litter boxes—an unusual but not unheard of situation.

The result, of course, was that no self-respecting cat would share a bathroom with a toy poodle. Or a German shepherd. Or an Irish wolfhound. It didn't matter where you were from. This was a private bath.

The solution was simple. We jerryrigged the door of the "cat" room with a chain that kept the door ajar so only the cat could fit through, then provided Pepi with his own litter box. This made Pepi very happy. He was pretty sure he was the only poodle in the neighborhood with his own private litter box.

The Crookshanks even put a little sign on his box: NO CATS ALLOWED!

CAT NIPS

- Don't overlook any details in your description of a behavior problem. The smallest thing can be important. I know—I've overlooked them, myself.
- Kitty litter is for kittens/cats; puppy litter and pads are for puppies/small dogs. If you require an alternative to walking your dog, check out this option at your pet store.
- If your cat leaves urine or feces next to the litter box, he's sending you a message: "I've come to use the box and there's something I don't like. Now it's your job to figure out what it is."

- Three or four clumps of urine per twenty-four hours is normal. Only two clumps? I'd get very suspicious. One clump or none? Start looking around the house.

- The important definition of a clean litter box is not your definition. It's the cat's.

- Remember, cats like a "flushed toilet"—just like people do.

Chapter 3

FRITZ THE SPRITZ

Why did Mr. Hogworth's Sunday suit need to go to the dry cleaners every Monday morning? Because it was wet, of course. Yes, wet! Courtesy of Fritz, the cat, who managed to find the dark blue wool suit wherever Mr. Hogworth put it. Draped over a chair? ZAP! Full of cat urine. Hung on a doorknob? ZAP ZAP! Thrown on the bed? ZAP ZAP ZAP!

When Mr. Hogworth came home from church, Fritz would follow him around the house, almost stalking him. He even hissed at him. This would have scared the pants off Mr. Hogworth, but he was afraid to get undressed.

Oh, and things got even stranger....

Once a week, Fritz turned his attention from Mr. Hogworth to his fourteen-year-old daughter, Melissa, stalking her around the house, throwing in an occasional hiss, jumping on the furniture around her, and standing his ground, as well as urinating on her clothes she had strewn on the floor.

That's when I got the call.

No, it wasn't a typical litter box problem. The Hogworths kept the boxes clean, and Fritz used it on a regular basis, with those two major exceptions.

This was a mystery. Why would a perfectly normal cat

stray from his habitual litter box routine only for these two very specialized circumstances?

Remember that while dogs get a lot of credit for having super noses, a cat's sense of smell is nothing to sneeze at. Cats are every bit as sensitive to odors, and their behavior can often be affected by new or unusual smells.

Was there something about that suit that set Fritz off, or did he just love navy flannel? We experimented with a number of different clothes placed on the bed, on a doorknob, and on the dining room chairs. Incredibly, Fritz was very apparel-specific. He liked the blue flannel. Or he *hated* the blue flannel. It depends on how you look at it.

Once I established that, it was pretty easy to figure out. It was unlikely that the color of the suit mattered, but maybe that suit had a different odor. Why? Because that was Mr. Hogworth's Sunday attire, and it was the only time during the week that Mr. H. threw on a dab of his new Christmas cologne—before going off to services. That cologne had a very musky scent, the kind of aroma that reminded cats of—what else?—other cats. Fritz was just leaving his calling card.

Now what about Melissa? She used perfume all the time, so why wasn't Fritz on a constant prowl after her? Why only once a week? This was simply a matter of finding some connection between the days that Fritz was piddling and spraying on Melissa and some specific pieces of clothing or aggressive action toward the teenage girl.

On an additional call I learned things had gotten worse. One time when Melisssa was petting Fritz in her lap, he left a little "present" on her new riding outfit. There are a number of clues in that last sentence if you're looking to solve this mystery.

The riding outfit was a Christmas present to go along with horseback riding lessons, lessons that Melissa went to each week as faithfully as her dad went to church. Horse odor would not generally create a problem for a cat. Their scent is neither a threat nor a form of communication. But the mystery was solved when I learned that the horse stables were thick with cats—mascots to the horses and pets of the stable hands.

Needless to say, Melissa had befriended the cats as well as the horses, and their scent was pretty strong on her clothing when she returned from her lessons. Whoever those cats were that Fritz smelled, he wanted to communicate with them. Remember, urination is a form of communication for felines.

In this case, the answer was pretty clear. Melissa needed to leave her riding clothes in the garage and bathe before playing with Fritz, and Mr. Hogworth needed to either give up cologne or hang his suit up. Mrs. Hogworth didn't think he was capable of either, but when she told him that was what the doctor ordered, he complied.

Everybody was happy. Especially the people at church. The people in the pew next to Mr. Hogworth weren't crazy about the cologne either.

CAT NIPS

- New odors can be challenging, even threatening, to a cat. Remember: A cat's sense of smell is about thirty times more powerful than ours.

- The odor of another cat can be threatening to a cat.

Chapter 4

HONEY DO LIST

Honey was no ordinary cat.

Actually, she *was* an ordinary cat. That's what makes this case so interesting.

Honey's owner originally called because when she returned home from work each day, she found cat feces all over the house. Not in any particular area, but everywhere. Feces under the dining room table, under the couch, in the corner of the living room, under the coffee table. If feces had been eggs, this would have been a heck of an Easter hunt.

"What about the litter box?" I asked. "Any waste in there?"

"Only urine," came the reply.

Then I asked if the feces had any kitty litter on it. In other words: Had the waste started in the box and then been taken out? The answer was complicated by the fact that the owner was using a kind of kitty litter that did not cling to the rather dry feces. But I was hoping to determine if the cat was using the litter box or was avoiding it altogether. My guess was that the cat was not using the box, a somewhat common problem that I had seen frequently.

To my surprise, after close owner inspection, she discovered that the waste did have litter on it. Which meant the cat *was* using the box.

If the cat was using the box, and the waste was all over the house, the cat must have been batting the stuff around like a soccer player on uppers. Cats, as a general rule, will not pick up feces with their teeth.

I envisioned Honey doing her business, then swatting the "little gems" from the litter box with a perfect forehand and playing kick the can with her waste material all through the house. The implication of this brought a smirk to my face, which made me glad I did my diagnosis on the phone. Honey's owner would not have been amused.

Here's where a total pet history is important. As I continued to question Honey's owner, I learned she had not noticed the problem on weekends. This was a Monday-through-Friday occurrence, a little nugget of information that the client had not really paid much attention to.

Often, a behavioral diagnosis uncovers a slight change in a pet's routine, leading to a change in the way the cat or dogs behaves. This was a perfect example.

Why did this not occur on the weekends? Probably because Honey was exercised, chased about, and loved and petted on Saturdays and Sundays, but she was pretty much left to herself during the work week. She was, quite literally, bored out of her feline skull. With no video games or a good book to occupy her time, she turned to field hockey. Her puck was a little unorthodox, but it served its purpose. It gave Honey something to do.

Cats do love to sleep, often up to sixteen to twenty hours a day. But those waking hours require some stimulation. The difference between the attention Honey was paid on the weekends and the lack of activity during the week was too much of a contrast. So Honey created her own intramural sport.

I was pretty sure I had made the right diagnosis, but successfully achieving a solution is the only way to prove a theory. The goal here (excuse the expression) was to control the boredom and keep the feces in the box.

Both were easily accomplished. We substituted a litter box with higher sides, making her slap shot nothing but a volley off the side wall. If Honey wanted to play with feces, she'd have to entertain herself in a cramped arena.

And, of course, I encouraged Honey's owner to provide some additional cat toys when she was absent during the workday and to be particularly loving and playful when she returned home each evening.

That was the end of feline hockey. No more little pucks were found around the house, and Honey never spent any time in the penalty box—just the litter box.

CAT NIPS

- A well-exercised cat is a snoozing cat.

- Cat behavior is driven by environment and genetics. You can't change the genetics, so work on the environment. By the way, *you* are the environment.

- When working with your cat's behavior, expect the unexpected. If you could predict a cat's behavior, I wouldn't be in business.

Chapter 5

STINKING OUTSIDE THE BOX

My client, Elwood, was quite the ladies' man, or so he thought. In fact, every night before he got into bed there was a little message on his pillow from Tammy or Timmy.

These were not the attractive singles he met at Club Med; they were his cats. And the message wasn't a love note; it was a pile of feces or a puddle of urine.

And that wasn't the only message in the house. Elwood must have had call waiting, because he also had similar messages around (not *in*) the litter box. There were also a few reminders of feline inhabitance in the sink, on the shower floor, and in the bathtub. Elwood had found love in all the wrong places.

When Elwood called, he didn't know where to turn, which was understandable, because there was cat waste everywhere. In cases like this there are often some obvious explanations. For instance, the cat may have a urinary tract infection that results in pain during urination. When this happens, the cat associates the box with discomfort and then keeps searching for a "painless" place to eliminate.

More likely—actually, much more likely—is that the

owner of the cat or cats has never fully understood the fastidiousness of the feline. Elwood, like many people, was pretty meticulous in his own life. The average person will avoid a restroom stall where someone has failed to flush. Many people will hop back in their car and drive another sixty miles on the interstate if they find unclean bathrooms. Cats just sneak around the corner.

But back to Elwood. Like most cat owners who face this problem, Elwood thought he was cleaning the box enough, but, in fact, he was falling quite short. While every cat is different, a box should be cleaned three times a day—more often if you have multiple cats. The more boxes, the better. Would you buy a house with one bath? Would you flush once a day? Am I making my point?

Before Elwood called me, he had made a few futile attempts to control the problem. At one point, when he noticed the cats going in the kitchen sink, he had moved the litter box up on the counter. This is not only a violation of my recommendations, it's probably not something the Board of Health would recommend, either. Of course, Elwood did change the litter when he first moved the box, which permitted the cats to have a few return visits while everything was clean. Elwood thought he had solved the problem, but the next day it was time to rinse out his sink again.

Even if you clean the litter box, once a cat has found a new special place, it may be a little more difficult to dissuade him from returning to the scene of the grime. In the case of the bed, I suggested a shower curtain instead of a bedspread. Cats do not like to feel the urine under their feet; they like the moisture to be absorbed. That's why the man who invented kitty litter is up there with

Bill Gates and the guy who invented the wheel.

It did finally sink into Elwood's head that the dirty litter box was the origin of his problem, and the proof was that as soon as he cleaned the boxes, the cats were waiting in line to use the facilities.

Elwood also realized that the dirty pillow should have been the first indication to him that something was wrong. Remember, Elwood was a ladies' man, but he probably didn't share our conversations with his girlfriends.

Oh, if pillows could talk.

CAT NIPS

- Why would your cat quit using his litter box? Why would you quit your job? Failed expectations, that's why.
- If you doubt your cat wants his box cleaned, watch him watching you cleaning it. He can't wait.
- You can't change your cat's brain. But you can change his litter box.

Chapter 6

LITTER MATES

Why does an ailing cat not urinate or defecate in his box?

Why would a perfectly healthy cat avoid urinating or defecating in his box?

The feline world is just littered with mysteries like this.

When Angela called about her cat Sasha, it was important to know right from the start that Sasha was diabetic. That kind of information can be crucial in understanding and diagnosing a behavioral problem. The vast majority of my clients and their pets have been referred by their veterinarians, who have examined and ruled out or corrected relevant medical problems.

Yes, Sasha was a diabetic. But did that explain why she always put feces in the box, but was urinating in the bathroom sink periodically? Maybe. Maybe not. Angela was a registered nurse and quite adept at giving Sasha her daily insulin injections, but she was hard-pressed to explain Sasha's porcelain potty preference. Angela also told me that Sasha had, on more than one occasion, urinated right in front of her in the sink.

Before I assumed there was any relationship between the diabetes and the litter box problem, I went through my usual discussion about having at least two boxes, located in different areas, for each cat. Frequent cleaning of the boxes makes a difference in many cases like this, but for Sasha the additional box and more frequent cleaning made little difference. Sometimes, when Sasha had to go, she got that *sinking* feeling no matter how many boxes there were.

When cats are sick, litter box decorum is many times the first thing to go. A cat who is suffering from constipation, for example, might associate the box with the pain from defecating. The cat's refusal to use the box is really his way of saying, "It hurts when I go here; maybe it won't if I go over there." The same can be said upon the pain of urination when there is a urinary tract infection.

But was the diabetes related to the problem? This required a little investigation, so the next time Angela called and started talking about this problem, I asked her to put a cork in it. The sink, that is. By trapping the urine, I could have Angela take a sample and test it for its glucose level to determine if Sasha was receiving the correct amount of insulin.

As I predicted, Sasha's urine was out of sync (and soon would be out of *the* sink). Her failure to go in the box and her boldness in having an accident right in front of Angela was, I believe, a form of communication. Both cats and dogs use urine to "talk" to others—not just to other animals, but to their caretakers, as well. Sasha's behavior reflected the stress and distress that she was feeling. She wanted Angela to know she was not feeling well.

•••••••

It was only a few months later that I received a call from another distressed pet owner with a similar problem. Mrs.

Heller informed me that one of her two cats was diabetic. And one of her two cats was urinating and defecating next to the box, rather than in it. Based on the previous case, the explanation was pretty straightforward. Or so I thought.

Mrs. Heller was claiming that Bolivar, the diabetic cat, was meticulous about urinating in the box numerous times a day. It was Simon, the healthy feline, who preferred perimeter shooting.

I told Mrs. Heller that diabetic cats produce more urine so more boxes are required, but I was quickly assured there were boxes galore in the house. At my insistence, Mrs. Heller increased the frequency of cleaning the boxes to three times a day, which did improve the problem, but it did not completely end it. There must have been another reason. I suspected a twist on the case described above and asked Mrs. Heller to have her veterinarian check Bolivar's urine for glucose levels. Bingo, an unacceptable level was found; the cat's insulin level needed to be increased.

Here was a case where the ailing cat was comfortable going in all the boxes, but he was also sending a message. And the recipient of that message was Simon. When Simon approached the boxes, he detected an unexpected and unhealthy odor. That was enough to disrupt his normal routine. Not wanting to go into a contaminated box, Simon searched for another, but all the boxes had been tainted by Bolivar. Therefore, he eliminated on the floor next to the box.

Once Bolivar's system was correctly regulated, the cats started sharing the boxes again. I am convinced that this was a kind of low-tech communication between the two cats and their owner that something was amiss.

After that, whenever Simon eliminated next to the box, Bolivar was taken to the veterinarian to have his insulin level adjusted. Mrs. Bolivar now realized how cats can communicate with their urine.

Let's just call it pee-mail.

CAT NIPS

- It's very difficult to modify behavior that is driven by a medical problem. That's why your veterinarian is so important.
- When cats are ill, they will not risk contaminating themselves by returning to a dirty litter box.
- Cats have a unique way of communicating with you. Take the time to get on their wavelength.
- Replace litter boxes yearly. They become sour. You may not smell it, but your cat will.

Chapter 7

WRATH OF A SALESMAN

As a veterinarian who limits his practice to animal behavior, I have learned a great deal about feline elimination behavior. And I know a lot about kitty litter. The different substrates, textures, odors, and consistencies of kitty litter have been studied ad nauseam. I wouldn't be surprised if someday someone writes a doctoral dissertation on kitty litter. If I were writing it, I'd call it: "The Effect of Various Litter Types on Cat Elimination Behavior." Dick Wolfsie, my co-author, said he'd call it: "A Feces Theses."

Yes, it's another litter box story. It started like all litter box cases, a call from a client who couldn't understand why her cat, Merlin, would occasionally avoid the litter box, defecating on the carpet in the dining room. But the rest of the time, Merlin was right on target.

At this point you pretty much know the checklist I go through. I confirmed the feces were of normal consistency and that Merlin had been examined by a veterinarian and was in good health.

It appeared to me that Merlin's owner, Gloria Cassidy, was pretty knowledgeable when it came to managing litter boxes and had provided a very appealing opportunity for Merlin to use the facilities properly. This problem required thinking *outside* the box.

It was during our next conversation that things came into focus.

"Dr. Sampson, Merlin didn't put feces in the box at all this past weekend. And this is a real problem for me, because my fiancé moved in a few weeks ago and he's never said so, but I don't think he's crazy about cats to begin with. What I'm feeling right now is, 'Love me, love my cat.'"

Oh, the little smirk that crept across my face. Gloria had possibly provided the clue I had been looking for. But it required a bit more exploring to confirm my suspicions. When I learned that her fiancé, Eddie, was a traveling salesman, I pursued this issue in our next phone call.

"Think back, Gloria. Is there any connection between when Merlin avoids the box and when Eddie is home from one of his business trips?"

As usual, it was the five seconds of dead silence on the end of the phone that indicated to me that I had hit upon something.

"Come to think of it, that does seem to be when it is happening. Last Saturday morning, Eddie smelled something odd, jumped out of bed, and stepped right in it. He was steamed."

And poor Gloria, a cat person, was also about to step into it—step into a relationship with a man who was *not* a cat person. I'm no marriage counselor, but this can mean stress in a relationship. It certainly meant stress for Merlin. I don't know how long it took Gloria to discover that Eddie didn't like cats, but I can assure you that Merlin knew it first.

Eddie was never mean to the cat, but he was very

indifferent and unresponsive. Merlin was not really looking for constant attention, but cats are very sensitive to human emotions. Cats are not spiteful—that's a human quality—but stress-driven anxiety is a pretty good motivator of this kind of inappropriate behavior. And in cats, the first casualty is often the litter box.

It was time to make Eddie a cat person—or at least to make him an even better salesman. We figured if Eddie could sell life insurance to college students, he could convince Merlin that he was his new best friend.

When he was home, Eddie became the sole feeder of Merlin, which was great because Merlin's favorite food was sole. He gave Merlin treats whenever he entered the house, and slowly but surely both man and feline began playing together. Gloria was to limit her attention toward Merlin, driving Merlin to Eddie for attention. Whatever Eddie was selling, Merlin was buying it. Within weeks, Merlin not only had warmed up to Eddie, and vice versa, but the cat became the official door greeter, anticipating more wonderful cat people just like Eddie who would provide treats and attention.

And what about my plan to stop Merlin from making deposits on the carpet? Did it work? Like magic.

CAT NIPS

- Why do cats often prefer the dining room when they pass up the litter box? Because most dining rooms are rarely used and have two means of escape.

- You're a cat person, but your new boyfriend is not. Good luck!

- A change in the consistency of your cat's feces (too hard or too soft) may cause her to avoid her box.

Chapter 8

BOX TOPS

Thelma and Clyde were good pet owners, but they kind of forgot that while they were aging, so were their three cats. The cats' litter boxes had been pretty functional early on; both were the covered variety, the ones with a fitted lid. I am not generally in favor of beginning with a box like this, but some cats are shy about their constitutional moments, and once you start with a covered box, it's sometimes hard to change. Stand by for proof.

Of the three cats, Joker was the most arthritic, and the box he had opted to use over the years was accessible only through a small opening, where, once inside, it was difficult for the fifteen-pound feline to maneuver. The other two cats, Spunkie and Tuffy, were also past middle age, but they were faring a little better. At least so far.

As it became increasingly difficult for him to use the covered box, Joker, who was literally a creature of habit, came up with an innovative solution to his dilemma. Forgoing the box altogether was unbecoming, so Joker split the difference. Instead of going into the box, he just stuck his head in the entry hole, then eliminated on the floor surrounding the box. If it hadn't been so unpleasant to watch, it would have been funny. Actually, it *was* pretty funny. For about a week.

Meanwhile, Spunkie and Tuffy had problems of their own. The boxes were not being kept as clean as they should have been, in part due to the aging owners' limited ability to change the litter frequently enough for three large cats. When the boxes got dirty, the duo started using various corners of the room. The result was that Thelma and Clyde were doing a lot of bending over. At least they were starting to understand some of Joker's issues.

I had Thelma and Clyde buy a couple of large plastic storage boxes, about thirty inches long, eight inches wide, and six inches deep. I recommended that the top be left on one old box so as to make the transition to topless boxes a little easier. As I noted earlier, habits are hard to break. Especially cold turkey. I wanted the cats to have an option.

Because I urged Thelma and Clyde to keep both boxes extra clean by scooping the litter several times a day, Spunkie and Tuffy easily made the transition, ultimately using both new boxes. They weren't used to such clean accommodations, and they liked the improved conditions.

But Joker was a tough nut to crack. He had gotten so used to his head in the hole that even though the new boxes had lower sides and room to move inside, Joker still opted to stick his head in the covered box and do his business on the floor. Thelma and Clyde still were not laughing. But we know you are.

Solving this problem required a little constructive—actually, constructional—thinking. If Joker wanted to stick his head in the hole, who were we to stop him? We placed a very shallow traditional litter box in front of the portal. Joker easily negotiated the rim, stood in the litter, stuck his head in the hole, and did his business. He was right on target, right in the middle of the kitty litter. Maybe I should get the Purr-litzer Prize for that idea.

The point of this story is that cats develop very personal prejudices about kitty litter and boxes. That's why so many stories in this book are about kitty litter and boxes. Many a cat's psychological and medical issues are written in the sands of litter. Be a good interpreter of these messages, and it will go a long way toward understanding your cat.

While some bad litter habits must be corrected or broken, solutions to problems should take into account the habitual nature of cats and make necessary accommodations, as we did with Joker.

The next time circumstances require that you use a Porta Potti and you wish you could stick your head out the window, think about Joker. This will bring a big grin to your face—something that doesn't happen very often in a Porta Potti.

CAT NIPS

- When cats grow older, they become more fastidious about their bathroom habits. People do, too—you'll see (if you haven't already)!

- If your cat is stressed, a change in his litter box habits may be the clue.

- Senior citizens shouldn't have to climb stairs to eliminate, sleep, or eat. Neither should old cats.

- Use only hot water to wash the litter box. Some cats dislike cleanser odors. And they are just looking for an excuse to go elsewhere.

Chapter 9

CHEESE WHIZ

Bartles and Jaymes were two cool cats. Which is why they were named after wine coolers, I guess.

The Bindermans had never had a lick of trouble with the two brothers, although Bartles was well known in the neighborhood for displaying his rodent catches at various neighbors' front doors.

Then one frosty Sunday winter evening while the Bindermans were watching an old movie, Bartles walked to the TV set, looked up at them, and urinated right in front of Humphrey Bogart on the brand-new Berber carpet.

Mrs. Binderman had a low tolerance for the unexplainable, and minutes later she called my home office to report the incident. When I saw the message light on my answering machine, I was intrigued. Behavior issues are important, but most develop over time and can wait until the next morning.

Mrs. Binderman was utterly perplexed. Both brothers had—excuse the expression—a spotless record in the litter box category lately, so what would have prompted such an overt digression from the norm?

When I returned the call, I learned that Bartles had once suffered from a urinary tract infection, and since this disorder occasionally recurs, I suggested that Mr. B. immediately put Bartles in the bathroom with his litter box and see their veterinarian first thing in the morning. If Bartles was in pain, we wanted to ensure relief as soon as possible and get him back in the litter box so that his discomfort would not be associated with the litter and the box any longer than necessary. In the meantime, I had Mrs. B. check around and confirm what I had suspected: Bartles had left several puddles around the house in search of a place where urinating would not cause him pain. He was still looking and decided to get their attention regarding his problem.

Bartles was again treated and cured of his urinary tract infection, but, as is sometimes the case, he still avoided the litter box, which in his mind had been connected with the burning he felt when eliminating. Bartles even urinated on the linoleum floor of the laundry room when confined, which confirmed his distrust of the box.

I had Mrs. B. replace the two boxes with new large plastic storage boxes, experiment with varying litters, and even move the boxes to a different room, all in the hopes of creating a fresh start for Bartles by deemphasizing the connections he had made with the old box. We also added additional boxes, in case having to share a box with Jaymes might have contributed to the problem.

This all seemed to have little effect, but the Bindermans did report that when they placed Bartles by his box and gently cajoled him into entering, he seemed less anxious and often complied. With that in mind, I upped the ante a bit and suggested a small cube of cheese as a reward when he completed his "business."

At the time, it seemed like a great idea.

Oh yes, Bartles loved that cheese. So much so that he became a regular box visitor, and when he went he made quite a bit of clatter to ensure that all who were listening knew he was hard at work. When he completed his task, the Bindermans stood by waiting to present the reward.

It still sounds like a great idea, doesn't it?

Bartles soon became a cheese whiz, greeting the Bindermans at the door when they arrived home, then dashing off to the box, where he made the appropriate clamor and soon received his incentive.

Are you starting to see anything wrong with the idea?

Then the Bindermans noticed that when Jaymes went in the box to eliminate, Bartles would go in right behind him and re-cover the urine clumps, pop out of the box, and expect a treat.

Hmmm! No idea is perfect, you know.

Then the Bindermans called to tell me that Bartles was waking them at two o'clock every morning to notify them he was getting ready to use the litter box, so they had better get ready to cough up the cheddar. The Bindermans hadn't had a good night's sleep in a week.

Okay, maybe this was not such a good idea, after all.

But the carpet *was* dry.

I did get a Christmas card from them the following year with Mr. and Mrs. Binderman cradling Bartles and Jaymes in their arms. Everyone was smiling. Even the cats.

The photographer must have said, "Say cheese."

CAT NIPS

- Reinforce acceptable behavior with intermittent treats. Anticipation is a powerful force.

- What makes a great litter box? Plastic storage boxes, thirty inches by eighteen inches by six inches.

- Why is your cat pawing at wet carpet? Possibly to cover up your other cat's misdeed. Interesting, huh? Find the real culprit.

- Some cats are spooked by the sound of washers and dryers, yet the laundry room is the most common place for keeping litter boxes.

Chapter 10

CALLED ON THE CARPET

The Flanagans truly loved their cat, Mitzi, but they were about ready to throw in the towel. I wish they had. It would have made my job a lot simpler. I'll explain in a moment.

Mitzi was a three-year-old black fraidy-cat who had, at the age of one, endured a painful battle with a urinary tract infection.

As is many times the case, Mitzi associated the pain she was feeling when urinating with the litter and the litter box. The result was she had not used the box for that bathroom activity in almost two years, opting instead to urinate on the rug in her room where the box was located and where the Flanagans fed her and left her toys. Because the Flanagans had planned on moving anyway, they accepted this behavior and simply cleaned up after Mitzi. Mitzi did defecate in the box—not so unusual, really, because there had been no pain associated with that activity while she was sick.

If you have ever had a cat declawed, you may recall that the veterinarian recommended you dispense with the traditional litter during the healing process. Oftentimes, shredded paper is suggested as an alternative. Traditional litter can cause pain or get into the surgical site and cause infection, but there is another reason. Any discomfort that the litter causes the cat's healing paws may cause the cat to associate her litter and box with pain. If that happens, you can end up with a cat like Mitzi, who avoids the box because she associates elimination in the litter with pain.

The Flanagans were getting ready to make a switch to a new home. Usually, I don't like being called on the carpet, but this was the very reason for their call. Was it possible, they wanted to know, to change Mitzi's habits after two years? Could I get her to urinate in the box instead of on the carpet?

We chose the laundry room, an area with a shiny new linoleum floor, to confine Mitzi day and night for a little experiment. This was perfect for our trial, because cats hate urinating on hard surfaces. The urine runs under their feet, a feeling they detest. And if a cat will go on linoleum, you know she will go on carpet. We didn't want her to have access to the carpet. It was a new house, remember.

We needed to determine if Mitzi's avoidance of the litter box was because of negative feelings about the litter, about the box, or about a combination of the two. Establishing that can help solve the issue, so the first thing we did in the new home was rotate the boxes with different kinds of litter to see if a new texture or consistency would attract her. Only one box was put out at a time. We tried several, including conventional clay, silica, paper, wheat, corncobs, wood shavings, and even peanut shells. You name it, they bought it. In fact, because Mitzi was originally an outdoor cat, we even imported some soil from the woods.

Despite all her choices, Mitzi still urinated on the linoleum floor. Every time. No exceptions. She continued to defecate in the second box of clumpable clay litter, which we always kept in the laundry room to ensure she retained that good habit.

This begged the question of whether it was the box or the litter that she disliked. I suggested that the Flanagans take the different litters out of the box and place them in small piles on the hard floor. No change. She still urinated on the floor.

It was then that we finally threw in the towel. Literally. Generally, I do not suggest a fabric like this as a substitute for kitty litter because it is too much like carpet, the very fabric we didn't want Mitzi to urinate on.

I had the Flanagans spread a small hand towel on the linoleum floor. I remember waiting for the next phone call.

"It worked. Mitzi will urinate on a towel. By the way, Dr. Sampson, are we happy about this?"

I explained to the Flanagans that while it was not a typical solution, I had had cases like this before. And there were some advantages. All the Flanagans needed were a pile of small towels, a water bucket, and a washing machine. In some ways, it's easier than cleaning up litter. They liked the idea.

Our next step was to take the towel off the floor and place it in the litter box. No litter, mind you, just the hand towel. Once again, Mitzi seemed comfortable with the new arrangement and happily urinated on the towel.

But now that she liked towels, would she urinate on the rug when released in the house? When the Flanagans were home, I had them monitor Mitzi when she was lose in the house, slowly increasing the amount of time she was allowed to roam free, then returning her to her room, where she could urinate on the towel in the box. The Flanagans needed to be confident that Mitzi would not urinate on the rug. When the Flanagans were sleeping, Mitzi was confined to the laundry room. Over time, Mitzi was allowed to have the run of the house because she was returning to the laundry room to use her towel.

It is very common for cats to be programmed to certain areas and textures, so the more she used the towel in the box, the more apt she would be to return to the laundry room to eliminate. Cats are creatures of habit.

The Flanagans were so pleased with the results, they had a housewarming party to show off their new house. I have been told that during the party they told this story to all their friends.

Maybe that's why no one used the guest hand towels.

CAT NIPS

- If you must change litter material, keep a box of the original available. Don't lose what you have gained.

- When moving to a new home, confine the cat to one room with food, water, and a litter box. When he is comfortable in this room, slowly expand his world.

- Cats that have had exposure to the outside may prefer soil to kitty litter. Good news: It's cheaper. Bad news: It's harder to clean.

- Cats have definite preferences in the kitty litter department. It will be easier for you to meet their needs than to change their minds.

Chapter 11

IT COMES WITH THE TERRITORY

Robert was a bobcat. That's right, a bobcat. I think the McPhersons changed his name to Robert because they thought it would make him sound more civilized. You need to do more than that. You can take the Bob out of bobcat, but he's still a cat, and a wildcat at that. Where they found him, I don't know. I don't recommend this type of pet, I just answer the phone and try to help people.

Ron and Annie McPherson, who lived in a palatial home outside of Chicago, also had two domestic cats, and all three felines got along beautifully. Nevertheless, when the McPhersons were gone for the day (and at night) they opted to keep Robert alone in the indoor pool area where he could not wreak havoc on curtains and rugs, which he had a tendency to do.

As Robert matured, the McPhersons were alarmed by what they told me was a growing aggressiveness toward their other two cats and toward them, along with a failure to eliminate in the box. Robert was marking his territory around the pool area. In general, Robert was antsy and anxious. These behaviors were disconcerting, because considering his origins, Robert had been pretty much a success story so far. "Why would things change all of a sudden?" the McPhersons asked me.

Unknowingly, the McPhersons had created this problem. Maybe a twinge of guilt had led them to place Robert in the glassed-in pool area where he could commune with nature. As he peered outside, Robert was often treated to a parade of wildlife that included birds, raccoons, rabbits, possums, squirrels, and even an occasional fox.

Poor Robert was not born to be raised in a closed-in pool area. Every fiber of his body was programmed to interact with (okay, kill and eat) many of the animals he saw marching by. Robert's nose also got a whiff of the procession through the glass doors. Talk about frustrating.

Here was an issue with a relatively easy solution. Robert needed to be cut off from that stimulation by moving him to an interior room, away from nature. The outside activity had raised his territorial and hunting instincts and increased his stress level. Stimulation, at least this kind, was the last thing Robert needed.

Robert calmed down within a couple of weeks, so much so that he was soon sleeping in the McPhersons' bedroom with the other two cats and even accompanied them on their sailboat on Lake Michigan and other trips. Talk about a conversation starter!

The McPhersons' two domestic cats would have been uninterested in the fauna of the area. They would, however, have been motivated by other domestic cats hanging around the pool area. Which leads to the story of Pudi…

Pudi was a twelve-year-old domestic cat, another feline who enjoyed the comforts of a nice home and whose owner fed stray cats of the neighborhood on her porch outside the glass-enclosed sunroom. She also wanted Pudi to commune with nature and have friends.

In a previous conversation, I told her that this activity can sometimes create problems. My clients employ me to give advice, but they don't always take it.

Sure enough, Mrs. Ellington called a few months later in a tizzy. Pudi, who had always been easy to deal with (I'm tempted to say, "was Pudi in her hands") had gone on a rampage. Pudi was defecating in the house as well as spraying the doors and windows with urine. The Ellingtons needed a lot of Windex.

What happened? Simple, really. Pudi, like Robert above, had seen a nice slice of life through the glass doors, but, unlike Robert, Pudi had no interest in her primal roots. What she did see one day was a new domestic cat that came to dine. That was too much for Pudi, who was willing to put up with a squirrel, raccoon, or bird but had no intention of letting another ordinary housecat claim any territory around her home. (This new cat, by the way, had strayed from Mrs. Ellington's neighbor's house next door. Their daughter, Terri, was home from college and had brought along a cat she found hanging around her dorm.)

We cut off Pudi's contact with the outside by blocking the glass doors with poster board. Pudi immediately returned to her litter boxes. A week later Terri went back to school with her cat. Out of sight, out of mind.

The dynamics between domestic cats are unpredictable. Sometimes a cat is driven nuts by one specific cat. Yet to a domestic cat, wildlife is pretty much window dressing.

For Robert the bobcat, the scenario was far different. Robert had made a pretty good adjustment to suburban living, but just under the surface was yearning to be wild and free. Bottom line: Either don't try to raise a cat like Robert, or recognize that you must isolate it from the untamed world.

Last I heard, Robert was doing fine. In fact, the McPhersons were still taking him on day trips in the car. There were some exceptions. Poor Robert never did get to see the Lincoln Park Zoo.

It's a good thing. There's only so much Windex in Chicago.

CAT NIPS

- I'm not wild about wild animals as pets. If you choose to have one, you will have to cater to some very special needs. Beware!
- If your cat is marking his territory, isolate him from the stimulus by confining him.
- Cats are always on the wrong side of the door. Or maybe you are.

Part Two

Aggression

"Kittens are born with their eyes shut. They open them in about six days, take a look around, then close them again for the better part of their lives." —Stephen Baker

"If a dog jumps in your lap, it's because he is fond of you; but if a cat does the same thing, it's because your lap is warmer." —Alfred North Whitehead

Chapter 12

99% CAT FREE

Mrs. Rossbottom's skinny little cat, Yogurt, had a problem. Actually, I came to discover that Mrs. Rossbottom had the problem and it kind of rubbed off on Yogurt. This in itself is not that unusual. I have stressed throughout this book that a lot of an owner rubs off on the pet. A lot of a pet rubs off on an owner, also, but that's mostly hair—and we had a much bigger problem here.

Mrs. Rossbottom was hyper and a bit insecure in her home. She was fearful of strangers, and the very sound of the doorbell—especially when it was someone unexpected—set her hair on end. Remember, I'm talking about Mrs. Rossbottom here, not the cat.

As time went on, Yogurt's behavior and personality began to mimic her owner's. When the doorbell rang, the cat became agitated, hissed, and attacked guests by swatting his clawless paw. Then to make matters worse, one morning after the bell rang Mrs. Rossbottom went to the door and stepped on Yogurt's tail. Mark Twain once said, "Even a dog knows the difference between being kicked and being tripped over." Apparently Yogurt never read Mark Twain (plus, she was a cat), so she promptly turned and sank her razor-like teeth into Mrs. Rossbottom's ankle. I know this scenario would have been funnier if Mrs. Rossbottom had been bending over.

And so began a downward spiral. Now Yogurt was even more fearful of the front door and anxious about the bell, which made Mrs. Rossbottom more uptight, which made Yogurt a little antsy and more aggressive, which made Mrs. Rossbottom paranoid, which made Yogurt.... Well, I think you get the picture.

Interestingly, Yogurt's response was very specific to the front door. A parade of people could come in the back way and Yogurt would pay little attention. To make matters worse, when a guest was heard at the front door, Yogurt was chased away, further agitating her and adding to the asocialization, and further reinforcing the negative doorbell experience.

The solution here was a clear case of counter-conditioning. Just like Pavlov could "unlearn" his dogs to salivate at a bell, I wanted Mrs. Rossbottom to condition Yogurt to respond more positively to the front door. This may appear easy, but most animals who suffer a negative experience are conditioned quickly and don't forget easily. This is not always the same for people. Ask someone who has been married three times.

We began by having Mrs. Rossbottom knock on the door and play with Yogurt in that area. We used a fishing pole with a feather, a laser light, and treats following play. This all had some positive effect, but not enough. Yogurt may have been low in fat, but she was high in anxiety.

I told Mrs. Rossbottom to always knock and come through the front door when she returned home and then give a treat to Yogurt, thus reinforcing the fact that positive things happened through that portal. The doorbell was disconnected to ensure that the sound would no longer have a negative trigger effect on Yogurt.

And visitors had to knock so intruders would not be associated with the ringing of the bell. Mrs. R. would answer the door and play with Yogurt.

This counter-conditioning took several months of very constant and repetitious work. The problem might have been cured sooner if Mrs. Rossbottom had not shared the same basic anxieties with the cat. There was a part of me that wanted to have someone play with Mrs. Rossbottom at the front door and give her chocolates when the doorbell rang so that her tension could be eased.

Here was clearly a case of a pet modeling behavior after its master. This is often a difficult cycle to break. I don't shy away from tough cases, but I will tell you this: If your spouse barks when the doorbell rings, there's not much chance of shutting up the dog.

CAT NIPS

- If your cat likes what you do for him, he will condition you to keep doing it.
- Use treats to motivate cats. Cats love treats as much as dogs. They just don't act as grateful.
- Cats are not submissive, so don't admonish cats directly. It causes fear and possibly aggression. And they will avoid you.

- Behavior modification requires patience, repetition, and consistency. This works for cats, dogs, and children.

Chapter 13

THE ODD COUPLE

Felix and Oscar were two indoor Burmese cats. With names like that you'd have to assume that there might be a few in-house squabbles.

Truth is that the two had gotten along famously, but then one day Oscar ambushed Felix—sucker-punched him, if you will. Without any apparent provocation, the older cat swooped down on Felix in a hissy-fit of historic proportions. Felix didn't know what hit him. And Mrs. Rodriquez didn't know what had prompted the attack.

The relationship between the two cats turned icy, to say the least. Felix was on his guard and, as the hair on his back bristled during each encounter, Oscar reacted in kind, even though it appeared as though Oscar had forgotten the original incident. "What's your problem?" Oscar seemed to be saying. "Okay, you wanna fight? Fine with me."

And fight they did. Big time.

Mrs. Rodriguez tried to be the mediator, but with little success. She also risked a painful cat bite. There was turmoil in the Rodriguez home. I was called to help restore domestic tranquility. I asked a series of questions to confirm my suspicions.

"Have you ever seen any other cats hanging around outside of the house? Is there a place in your house where the cats can see outside into the yard or street? Did Oscar ever show aggression toward you?"

As predicted, I got a "yes" to each question, confirming my initial hunch. This was case of *redirected aggression*. Here's what was happening:

The Rodriguezes lived in a small ranch house on a wooded lot. Mrs. Rodriguez confirmed that an occasional stray cat had peered through the family room sliding glass door. Oscar had peered back—and on a few occasions had tried to attack the other cat by lunging at the glass door. This encounter through the looking glass was at the root of Oscar's aggression. Cats are very territorial, and Oscar's turf was being invaded. The glass window prevented a normal venting of that tension. Instead, Oscar redirected his anxiety toward Felix, who had become the scapegoat. Many times the redirected aggression can focus on family members or the family dog. Cat bites can be serious, causing infection and pain.

The squabbles between Felix and Oscar would only wane if Oscar was not subject to the occasional intrusion of this other cat. It was important that all opportunities for a staring contest be eliminated. Drawing blinds and curtains is pretty useless, since a curious cat like Oscar can easily negotiate his wiry body between the window pane and the obstruction. I recommended poster board or decorative frost across all windows the cats looked out. Cats also can climb onto furniture to look out the window, so a total restructuring of the room is sometimes necessary. This may seem like a lot of work, but every encounter with that neighborhood cat would set the whole process back.

Of course, keeping other cats out of the yard is also helpful. Stop feeding birds, and remove catnip from the garden. A well-placed sprinkler, especially one with a motion detector, can do wonders to dampen the spirit of an inquisitive outside cat. If outside cats don't see your cat in the window, they take your home off the to-do list.

Now what about Felix and Oscar? Just waiting for them to be friends again was not an option—we needed to be more pro-active. The biggest mistake that people make in situations like this is to completely isolate the cats from each other, putting them in different rooms. The result is that tension builds slowly and their first encounter is, excuse the expression, cat-astrophic.

The cats did require separation, though. One was allowed to roam free and the other was restricted to a room, but the door to that room was tied with a shoelace attached to a nail in the door frame and to the doorknob to keep the door open an inch and a half. Now interaction was possible, replete with eye contact and the inevitable hissing and paw swatting, but there was no opportunity for a real squabble. The cats were rotated in the room to prevent territorialization. Over time, this would reduce their view of each other as threatening. To expedite this process, I suggested feeding both cats on opposite sides of the door.

Both cats needed exercise and more opportunities to play and interact, thus redirecting their anxious aggression. I had Mrs. Rodriguez swing a string with a toy through the cracked door to entice play and increase the cats' comfort level with each other.

If you're a pet owner, I will recommend exercise for almost every problem, kind of like chicken soup. It couldn't hurt. And it is usually a big help.

When it was time to reintroduce the cats, Oscar was tethered with a body harness and a six-foot nylon lead, serving as a constant reminder that he was being controlled. With the harness and lead anchored, the cats were allowed to be in each other's presence, reinforcing (for Felix, especially) that there would not be an attack.

Oscar and Felix slowly became friends again, but I recommended that the poster board or frost remain on the windows for a while to discourage stray cats from coming around. A new male cat had been seen wandering the neighborhood.

The last thing Mrs. Rodriguez wanted was a peeping tom.

CAT NIPS

- Cats are territorial when it comes to other cats. When it comes to dogs, squirrels, and raccoons, they could care less. Cats are good at caring less.

- Cat bites are painful and can cause a serious infection. Use a mop or broom to break up a cat fight. Then you can also use the broom or mop to clean up *after* the cat fight.

- If you or your cat has been bitten by a cat, take the wound seriously. There can be dangerous consequences from an untreated cat bite.

- If you don't want stray cats in your yard, don't feed birds or grow catnip. I didn't have to tell you that, did I?

- Many cats can take in excess of twenty-four hours to chill out after an aggressive encounter. Every cat is different. You can't change that. Be aware.

- A crack in a door that separates one cat from another is a window of opportunity—a window that allows interaction without the threat of an unpleasant encounter.

Chapter 14

LITTLE ORPHAN MANNY

When Sarah Gustafson adopted Manny the kitten at two weeks old, she said he had a face only a mother could love. But sadly, Manny never had a mother. Not for very long, anyway. Manny's mother was never cut out for mothering, so she just, well, cut out, to Timbuktu or Katmandu, or wherever cats go to escape the rat race—or get into one.

Happily, every one of Manny's brothers and sisters, all six of them, was adopted almost immediately. But sadly, every one of Manny's brothers and sisters was adopted almost immediately. Huh?

Yes, this is where the problem began—and it was a problem not too uncommon with what are called orphan cats.

Manny, like his orphan brothers and sisters at two weeks of age, required hand-rearing by his new owner. And because he was still a very young kitten, that included bottle feeding.

Mrs. Gustafson's heart had gone out to Manny, which was understandable, but when her hand went out to him, there was trouble. Big trouble. Mrs. G. first noticed an aggressive tendency when Manny was about six weeks old. He exhibited it when she returned home from work at the end of each day.

Manny just wanted to play. The problem? He didn't know how. Why? Because Manny had never been fully breast-fed by his mother nor had he had much opportunity to interact with his siblings, he had never learned how to inhibit and control his bite. Both dogs and cats learn early on what suitable play is through interaction with other members of the litter and their mothers. You bite too hard and you hear about it. You get bitten too hard, you express your displeasure. It's an invaluable learning process. Without it, dogs and cats would be rotten pets.

Part of the learning also comes from suckling. Mom lets any offspring know if the feeding is to aggressive. During a period of four to ten weeks, cats learn a great deal from Mom and from their feline family. Manny had missed six weeks of school.

And now as Manny reached twelve weeks of age, Mrs. Gustafson was feeling, quite literally, the results of Manny's deprived early childhood. Mrs. G.'s arrival home each night set Manny off. In his mind he was just playing, an explosion of unused energy, but the result was clearly aggressive in Mrs. G.'s mind. Mrs. G. was hurt in more ways than one. She was hurt because it seemed unfair that a cat she had devoted so much time to raising seemed to almost attack her. What also hurt was her hand, her ankle, and her leg, which Manny seemed to enjoy latching onto whenever Mrs. G. tried to offer some attention by petting or stroking him. When she first walked in the door, she was a moving target. And Manny seldom missed.

She turned for help to neighbors and friends, who offered her the very worst advice. "Flick his nose with your finger when he bites," said some. Others said to rattle cans of pennies or holler to frighten him. All bad advice. In fact, it was all counterproductive advice, making the problem even worse because it further excited the cat, causing him to want to play even harder. Remember, he didn't know how to play. But he sure did know how to bite.

The problem got worse and worse, and by the time the call finally came to me on Manny's four-month birthday, Mrs. G. was literally frightened of Manny. What might have been considered playful aggressiveness had clearly moved toward pure aggression.

I wanted most of Mrs. G.'s interaction with the cat to be indirect. I allowed an occasional pet or stroke with one finger under the chin or on the side of the face, but she was never to use her full hand down the neck or back.

Cats know human body parts and they know moving body parts. Felines are programmed to jump, catch, kill, and eat. So when Mrs. G. played with Manny by moving her hand under the covers, it may have protected her fingers, but it reignited his basic instincts to attack.

I wanted all play to be directed at interactive objects, like toys on fishing poles and laser beams. Under no circumstances was a part of Mrs. G.'s body to be used as a target. A box with a ping pong ball and objects hanging from doorknobs allowed Manny to work off some energy so that when Mrs. G. came home, she would not be the immediate focus of his energy. Instead, Mrs. G. went directly to the closet for one of several interactive toys and played with him.

All of these remedies had some effect, but this was a very difficult case. Biting cats are relatively uncommon. And the behavior of an orphan cat, like Manny, was especially tough to modify. If Manny did approach her or nip at her, Mrs. G. was to stand completely still. Cats are not interested in dead prey. When Mrs. G. did her statue impersonation, Manny usually lost interest.

Squirt bottles with a healthy stream of water are also very effective. In fact, I suggested she ready an entire arsenal of water dispensers so that there was ammunition in every room. Mrs. G. started carrying a bottle around on her belt so she was always armed and ready. All displays of aggression, even if intended as play, were to be suppressed with a stream of water smack in the face.

And finally, contrary to advice I give the vast majority of the time, I recommended an additional kitten. As a rule, adding a new pet to an existing problem is apt to stir up more trouble, but in this case, Manny needed a mentor and sparring partner—a new active kitten, a little older and a touch bigger, who could teach him the ABCs of playing and biting. Within a few weeks, the change was pretty dramatic. Not only was Fester teaching Manny how to play, but by the time Mrs. G. got home, Manny was too pooped to pounce.

Manny turned out to be a great little cat. His mother would have been proud. Wherever she was....

CAT NIPS

- If you have a behavior issue with your cat, adding a new cat will seldom solve the problem. This chapter's story is an exception.

- Orphan kittens require extra care. They missed out on having siblings and a mother. *You* are now the momma.

- Satisfy the prey-catching need in your cat by ending play with the toy landing on a treat so your cat can "kill and eat it."

Chapter 15

CAT WHO HATED CAMELS

There were three cats in the Simmons house: Otis, Molly, and Lilly. But when it came to Otis, there was no match. There were also no cigarettes. Otis stole and hid both. Here's the story.

Otis was a male cat, about five years old, who enjoyed playing with Lilly, although his play was decidedly rough. When he would engage in highly energized activity with Lilly, he would then direct that roughhousing to Molly, whose only mistake was walking into the room. In some cases, Otis would actually search out Molly to unload his unfinished aggression.

Mrs. Simmons was not immune to Otis's wrath, either. When she tried to pet Otis, possibly to soothe him, he would hiss, swat, and even bite at his owner. Convinced he needed a good lesson, Mrs. Simmons would clap her hands and holler at him. When that failed she smacked him or shook a can of pennies to frighten him. This seemed like a good idea at the time. It wasn't.

Mrs. Simmons's reaction sent Otis off to escape or hide, but he would often return a little later in the day and literally resume his attack on her or redirect the aggression toward Molly. Just like some people hold a grudge longer than others, cats can take quite awhile to cool down. You can play aggressively with dogs and in a few minutes most of them will be taking a nap. Not a cat. They are hard-wired and can stay aroused for hours.

Otis had reached the point where he would pay a visit to Mrs. Simmons's bedroom at night, hoping to complete their little to-do. That's when Mrs. Simmons called me. She was a bit unnerved. You couldn't blame her.

Otis was clearly a very manipulating cat—and a highly volatile one at that. Any petting of his body aroused him and, as noted, resulted in aggressive behavior, not just immediately, but for some time after.

And for reasons that we will never know, Otis was also a stealer. Among other things, he took Mrs. Simmons's cigarettes and hid them. He'd also take the matches. Cats are always trying to tell you something: Some cry for attention or food, others leave "messages" outside the litter box to communicate illness or anxiety. I couldn't decode this one, but the good news was it cut down on Mrs. Simmons's smoking, something her husband had not been able to get her to do. Interestingly, Otis didn't show aggression when Mrs. Simmons was smoking. He didn't even come in the room after she lit up. Did Otis hate smoke? Had he read the surgeon general's warnings? We'll never know. But he knew enough to hide the cigarettes. And the matches.

First, I suggested that Mrs. Simmons place a bell on Otis's collar. Plain and simple, Mrs. Simmons needed to know where he was and when he was on the prowl, so as to avoid any aggressive contact. Mrs. Simmons, as you may have guessed, had done it all wrong in her approach to Otis's aggression. Everything from clapping her hands to yelling to swatting and shaking a can of pennies had done nothing but heighten Otis's already anxious, almost hostile, state. Otis wasn't being taught to calm down; he was just being further antagonized and stimulated.

The trusty squirt bottle, delivering a stream of water to his face and saying nothing, was the best way to get Otis's attention without ratcheting up the aggression. Even this was a risk, but the cat did need to know his behavior would not be tolerated. The squirt bottle was employed whenever Otis played too assertively with Lilly or if his interaction with her had gone on so long that rough play was inevitable. Essentially, we were going to teach Otis how to play—how to appropriately have fun and exercise without getting overstimulated.

When Otis did play with Lilly, Molly was separated and placed in another room. We wanted to cut down on the redirected aggression. Mrs. Simmons was given very specific instructions on how to pet Otis, essentially avoiding full body strokes, but instead scratching under the chin or on the side of the face with one finger, which was nonstimulating.

Otis was forbidden in the Simmons's bedroom, isolated in his own bedroom at night and when the Simmons were gone. Once again, this is a case where we do not set a pet up to fail. It is better that Otis not have an opportunity to be violent than be punished for his bad behavior.

Otis did eventually come around, but a cat like this needs to be monitored carefully in order to control the play. Mrs. Simmons kept her squirt bottle at her side, watching Otis out of the corner of her eye. Mr. Simmons also kept a careful watch.

He smoked ten-dollar cigars.

CAT NIPS

- Physical punishment often escalates aggression in cats.

- If you don't shape your cat's behavior, he will shape yours. It's your decision.

- Cats are not submissive animals. If you want a guilty look, scold a Saint Bernard.

Part Three

Anxiety

"The cat is mighty dignified until the dog comes by."

—Southern Folk Saying

"The phrase 'domestic cat' is an oxymoron."

—George Will

Chapter 16

BY GEORGE!

George was a Siamese cat. He was also a Velcro cat. That's my analysis and I'm sticking to it. Most cats are pretty independent. With some, you get the feeling they can take you or leave you. And if they do take you, it's pretty much on their terms. Too much attention actually turns off some cats (see "A Stroke of Jeannie"). George was just the opposite.

George's caretaker, Mr. Lochart, was a traveling salesman, so he was often out of town, leaving the cat alone in the house. Upon his return, Mr. Lochart would discover that the cat was also a bit of salesman. George was leaving his samples everywhere he went. And he went pretty much everywhere: on the couch, on the bed, on Mr. Lochart's favorite chair.

My first inclination was to consider the simplest explanation. There is a saying in medicine: "Don't look for zebras when it may be horses." My analysis was that the cat's litter box was filling up and George, like most cats, simply needed a cleaner place to go. That should be an easy problem to correct. Pay the kid next door to come in twice a day, clean the box, set out fresh food, and play with the cat. Re-create as closely as possible the conditions that exist when Mr. Lochart is at home.

We tried that. It didn't work.

Soon after the first call, even when Mr. Lochart was gone only part of the day, George started to defecate or urinate out of the box. I was beginning to reassess my first thoughts when a call from Mr. Lochart clinched it. Mr. Lochart had been packing for a trip and left his suitcase open on the bed. George, like any good salesman, left his calling card, right after Mr. Lochart left the room. And right on top of Mr. Lochart's favorite tie.

This was not your usual litter box problem. It was a somewhat unusual case of feline separation anxiety. George loved Mr. Lochart in the worst way. And one of the worst ways a cat can love you is using (or in this case, not using) his litter box to communicate his feelings. In this case, George was a stressed cat.

Cats can read your behavior. They read signals better than a clean-up batter. And after a while George had associated Mr. Lochart's departure with the suitcases. Subsequent behavior and failure to use the litter box was not out of anger or spite, but due to stress. A more logical explanation is that the cat was marking areas to ensure his friend was guided home, creating a kind of signpost. That is why when Mr. Lochart left, George eliminated in areas where both had spent a significant amount of time: the bed, chair, desk, and couch.

My first suggestion was that we confine the cat to Mr. Lochart's home office with lots of toys. The space was small, but George would be comfortable there, having already spent many hours in that room when Mr. Lochart was working. Cats being territorial, he would establish his turf within the home. By defining the space, we could protect those areas where George was most apt to soil, like the desk chair, which we covered with plastic. The floors of the office were wood so George, like most cats, would probably not urinate there, disliking the moisture trickling under his paws.

When Mr. Lochart was home, all activity with George, like feeding and playing, was to take place in the home office. George could fall asleep in the "in box" on George's desk or take a snooze in the "out box." But he was always to have two clean litter boxes. This was George's new home. And because it was his defined territory, we were reducing the likelihood of his message-giving. When Mr. Lochart did go away, George felt more at home and possibly less abandoned.

I encouraged Mr. Lochart to play with George with interactive toys, fishing polls and laser lights, as often as possible because exercise is a very good de-stressor. I prescribed some antianxiety medicine initially. George was quickly weaned off medication, but it did give the behavioral treatment a jump-start.

And finally, I told Mr. Lochart never to pack his suitcase in front of George. We did not want George to stress out in anticipation of Mr. Lochart's departure, and we did not want Mr. Lochart's luggage flagged for a search at the airport.

Siamese feces, we feared, might be considered foreign contraband.

CAT NIPS

- To reduce stress in your cat, establish routines. Exercise will also reduce stress. If you find a routine that also results in exercise, you'll have killed two birds with… never mind, bad expression.

- If you suspect your cat has separation anxiety, don't make a big deal when you leave the house. Also, vary your departure. Use different doors, for example. Keep the cat guessing as to whether or not you are really leaving.

- If your cat suffers from separation anxiety, confining her to one room (which will essentially become the cat's room) goes a long way in preventing elimination throughout the house.

Chapter 17

HEATED DISCUSSION

When Arthur Higman, professor of English literature at a prestigious Indiana college, called to complain that his cat was urinating outside the litter box, I launched into a pre-set list of questions to be sure that the obvious had not been overlooked.

How many cat boxes are there in the house?
How often do you clean them?
Have you recently changed the type of litter you are using?
Have you moved the boxes?
How often is the elimination out of the box?
Does the cat use the box at all?

The professor was a bit put out. "I know how to take care of a cat, Dr. Sampson. After all, I am a professor of Litter-a-ture."

Yes, we've all had teachers like Professor Higman.

But there was one question that did pique the professor's curiosity. I asked if Pearl had ever urinated right in front of him, as if she were calling attention to her behavior.

"Why, yes, she has done that a few times. In fact, that's why I called you. She jumped up on my computer table and urinated on the printer while the pages of my new book were coming out."

I was tempted to say, "Everyone is a critic nowadays."

But instead I continued to listen. There was more to the story. Apparently Pearl was also going through a kind of needy stage in her life, a strange combination of demeanors that manifested in some very seductive rubbing against the professor's leg, excessive nuzzling, and constant purring (yowling might be a better word). At one point, Pearl had even snuggled up against the family dog—which was kind of odd, because Pearl never liked Waldo and Waldo never liked Pearl. Pearl was looking for love in all the wrong places.

It didn't take much more of this conversation to realize that I had neglected to ask a pretty basic question. My failure to do this probably reflected my hope that everyone recognized the importance of responsible pet ownership.

"Professor, has Pearl been spayed?"

"You mean like a eunuch in a Shakespearean play?"

Well, not quite, but at least we were starting to communicate.

Yes, Professor Higman had neglected to spay Pearl before her first heat. Being the classic absent-minded professor, he then completely forgot about this important obligation for cat owners. Of course, the professor also frequently forgot his coat, his keys, his wife's birthday, and to eat lunch.

But back to Pearl. Pearl was a housecat, and many people assume that spaying is not that important; after all, a queen does need a tom to reproduce. Even Professor

Higman understood this male/female thing. Heck, he had read *Romeo and Juliet* a hundred times. But there are other reasons to spay your female cat.

The results of this oversight are very predictable. Felines that have not been spayed are seasonally polyestrous, meaning their estrous cycles occur many times during certain times of the year—and sometimes as often as two or three times a month—until mated. Unbred cats become stressed, often meowing through the night. Even if the kitty is an indoor cat, you can expect some attempts at escape when you open the door. An unspayed cat is like a teenager who has been grounded. "Restless" would be an understatement.

Professor Higman was a bit embarrassed about the whole thing. He promised he would take Pearl to be spayed the next day.

Assuming, of course, he remembered where he parked his car.

Besides reducing the growing cat population, there are other benefits to spaying/neutering your cat:

In females:

1. Prevents cancer of ovaries and uterus
2. Reduces chances of mammary tumors
3. Prevents uterine infections

4. Reduces incidents of spraying to mark territory and/or attract male attention
5. Prevents heat cycles
6. Reduces roaming and aggressiveness
7. Population reduction and prevention

In males:

1. Eliminates the development of testicular tumors
2. Decreases incidences of prostate disease and cancer
3. Reduces chances of developing hernias
4. Reduces roaming and household restlessness
5. Reduces urine odor and incidents of spraying to mark territory
6. Reduces aggressiveness
7. Reduces roaming and territorialization
8. Population reduction and prevention

Chapter 18

OH BABY!

When the Beaglestaffs found clumps of black hair around the house, they were confused. Misty, their new bouncing baby girl, didn't have any hair. Mr. Beaglestaff didn't have hair any either. And Mrs. Beaglestaff was a blond. Usually.

The hair belonged to Patches, the Beaglestaffs' family cat, who was having the feline version of postpartum depression. Bringing a new baby home can be very disconcerting to a dog or cat that has in many cases occupied a rather lofty position in the family.

For Patches, it was particularly rough. First of all, Misty was the first child, so Patches had never dealt with a contender to her throne and, like many cats, was a creature of ritual. Patches slept in the same place each night (on the Beaglestaffs' bed) and enjoyed the predictable tummy rubs and cat play each evening after dinner.

Life was good. Until Misty pulled into the station.

Understandably, all eyes were now on Misty. All activity was focused on the new baby. All attention was lavished in a new direction. Mr. Beaglestaff understood why he was no longer being catered to, but Patches was perplexed, then downright angry. Her routine was out the window. Patches wondered if she was next.

It wasn't difficult to realize that every time that baby was around, Patches was in some way displaced. Because the baby slept in the Beaglestaffs' bedroom, Patches now ended up in the laundry room. When the baby was awake, Patches was either ignored or again put in laundry room. If the baby cried, Patches was stressed by the high-pitched sound. If she investigated the origin of the distress call, she was quickly picked up and put in another room. Patches was slowly going bald from her stress-related hair pulling.

Then one day Patches lunged at Mrs. Beaglestaff while she was tending to the crying, screaming baby. That led to a phone call to me. "The cat doesn't like the baby," Mrs. B. told me, "and I'm afraid she may attack the baby." While that is a bit uncommon, I understood her concern. Mrs B. was looking for some love and harmony in her family, and with all her new responsibilities she did not want to have to worry about her feline child, who by now had pulled out so much hair she had really earned the name Patches.

The way to handle this problem is to deal with it before it occurs. Many clients have called me before bringing their baby home, anticipating that the family pet might be upset by the newcomer. Many of my suggestions to the Beaglestaffs would have been that much more effective had they been instituted before the baby came home. Nevertheless, all was not lost.

The first thing was to prove to Patches that the very presence of the baby did not mean an unpleasant experience for her. I recommended that the Beaglestaffs completely ignore Patches when the baby was sleeping, but that they try to pay her more attention when the baby was awake. I recognize this is easier said than done, but a few pats and couple of treats every once in a while in the baby's presence is not that time consuming. I suggested that Mr. B. play with Patches while Mrs. B. was feeding the baby. The message was: "When Misty is in the picture, things look good for me."

When Mrs. B. used baby powder on her hands, she stroked Patches so the cat and the baby would have a similar aroma. Again, an important association: "Hey, she's petting me, and it smells like the baby."

The sound of crying is often disturbing to a pet, especially a cat. The noise is akin to a distress call. I suggested playing tapes of the baby crying even when the Beaglestaffs were not home. The audio was to be low so as not to be challenging, but it would accustom Patches to the sound. When the family was home, they could still use the tape, starting low and increasing the volume slightly. Again, those sounds were to be accompanied by some positive reinforcement of petting, playing, and treats.

Within a few weeks, Patches had pretty much been accustomed to the tape and the baby's actual crying and became more accepting of Misty. The biggest change in Patches was that after hearing the baby cry on and off all night, sleeping near a pile of dirty diapers, and smelling of baby powder, Patches realized motherhood was not for her. She even stopped pulling her hair out.

For the first time in her life, Patches was happy she was spayed.

Much of this story has been about a cat that was not prepared for a new arrival. Things would have been easier had the Beaglestaffs done a little preparing before the baby got home. The following suggestions should help any cat owner who is expecting a new addition to a family.

Rules for preparing a cat before a new baby comes home:

1. Any changes in the physical nature of the house, like new furniture and room arrangements, should be done gradually. Many cats are stressed by abrupt changes.

2. If your cat will require a change in where it sleeps, eats, or plays, do it weeks before the baby arrives. We do not want the cat to associate the change with the baby.

3. Bring objects that will be associated with the baby into the house as soon as possible. Blankets, cribs, and toys should all be in the house weeks before the child arrives. The less of a surprise the baby is, the better.

4. As noted above, any odors that you anticipate will be new, like baby oils, powders, bath soap, and dirty diapers, should be introduced as early as possible.

5. A tape of a baby crying may be played occasionally in various areas of the house, just so the sound is not a total shock the first time the pet hears it from the baby.

6. Walk around with a doll wrapped in a blanket along with the baby tape playing. This will help the cat become accustomed to this activity and reduce its stress when you must attend to the baby several times a day.

7. Any routine (like feeding, playing, and petting) in which you anticipate any change in the time, manner, or place should be altered slowly and long before B-Day.

8. The day you come home with the baby, allow the cat to see and smell him, if he is interested. Give the cat treats. Do not initiate direct contact at first. Repeat the process until the cat becomes comfortable in the room with the baby. Make sure every time the cat is around the baby, good things happen—petting, play, and treats.

CAT NIPS

Prepare for a new baby's arrival. Moms and dads need nine months. The cat can use two or three.

Chapter 19

THE BLUE WAVE

Unlike the general veterinary practitioner, I read journals to study the *behaviors* associated with medical conditions. That's why I occasionally identify behaviors that may have a medical origin and will frequently direct that client back to the referring veterinarian for a medical diagnosis confirmation and possible treatment.

Sometimes, the medical and behavioral aspects of the problem seem indistinguishable. That was the case with Blue, a six-pound Siamese cat who was exhibiting a growing obsession with his tail.

The Rudermans had noticed this slowly evolving over a period of time. Blue had been licking at his tail, then biting at it. The wounds became significant enough that they took him to their veterinarian, who treated the tail with steroids and antibiotics and gave Blue pain medication. When the problem continued and the tail became even more damaged, the veterinarian conducted a partial amputation with the hope that this would eliminate the source of the compulsive behavior. Blue would have a fresh, new (but shorter) tail.

Cases like these are tricky because it is often difficult to determine how the vicious cycle began. Many times we never find out. When Blue returned home, the hope was that his tail would no longer hold the same fascination as before, but sadly that was not the case. He continued to lick, bite, and gnaw at what remained of his appendage. It got ugly. Literally.

When the referral came to me, I tried a basic approach first, suggesting the Rudermans direct Blue's attention away from his tail by exercising him and engaging him with interactive toys. We even adopted the water bottle method, targeting a stream at Blue when he tried to gnaw at his tail. I also prescribed antianxiety medication, hoping to relax him and break the cycle. A follow-up call revealed there was some improvement, but not enough.

On further questioning, the Rudermans informed me that their stroking of Blue's neck and back occasionally set him off, igniting the tail biting, and the skin on Blue's back seemed to roll, almost in a wave, when he was sometimes petted. But it was hard to see because his hair was long.

It appeared as though the wave completed its cycle in the tail area, which resulted in Blue's frantic jump to the floor, and then the biting began. In fact, even if the cat was calmly sitting in their laps, they observed this skin-rolling phenomenon occasionally. When they saw it, they were not aware of its implications.

This condition is called hyperesthesia, a neurological disorder that is often referred to as pre-epilepsy. What we needed to do was shut down the abnormal activity of the central nervous system with anticonvulsant medication.

The primary cause appeared to be a medical disorder, but the hyperesthesia resulted in a cycle of self-abuse, which developed into an habitual behavior. That's why an antianxiety medication to address the compulsive aspect of this condition was also needed.

The Rudermans were instructed not to overstimulate the cat. All petting was to be confined to the head and chin area—no full-body strokes. And they were to make sure Blue got plenty of exercise with interactive toys.

There is no complete cure for this condition, but medication will control it. Observe your cat carefully, even while he is asleep, to detect any ticks or unfamiliar body twitches. If you see signs similar to Blue's, consult your veterinarian.

Remember, the patient can't report what's wrong or how he is feeling. Veterinarians (and pediatricians) depend on the owner's (or mother's) watchful eye to know there is something wrong. Your pet will let you know. You just have to be watching.

CAT NIPS

- Illness-driven behaviors are difficult to correct. That's why I frequently refer a client back to his veterinarian when I suspect this.
- Be a keen observer of your cat's behavior. Then you'll know when something is amiss.

Chapter 20

BORN TO BE WILD

Clouse never intended to have a huge family. He was born to be wild and was getting along pretty well on the outskirts of a wooded community, where he dined on mice and moles. Occasionally he ventured a little closer to civilization, where the Fairchilds often left food for feral cats like Clouse several hundred yards from their pricey three-level colonial home.

Sylvia Fairchild was a sucker for cats. It seemed that whenever she went to the pet store or the humane society (where she volunteered), she came home with another cat. And they saw her coming. The last time she was at the pet store, George, the manager, said that he had a cat with her name on it. That cat's name is now Sylvia. Sylvia was number twelve. Twelve cats and a big, lovable sheepdog named Greta. The Fairchilds had no children. I bet you could have guessed that.

Mrs. Fairchild did know something about cats. She knew enough to feed the feral population a fair distance from her home so that the wild felines would not accumulate around her property searching for food and send her own adorable dozen into a territorial tizzy.

For reasons I never fully understood, Sylvia Fairchild

had her eye on Clouse (she had names for all the cats who frequented her weekly kitty buffet). Maybe it was the way Clouse kept one eye on the food as he ate and the other on her as she sat in her car, watching. Maybe it was the fact that he was the most beautiful shade of charcoal gray, head to tail. Whatever it was, Sylvia wanted that cat. Sid, her husband, thought this was a mistake. If what Sid thought ever mattered, they wouldn't have had twelve cats. And a sheepdog.

Long story short, Sylvia Fairchild captured Clouse. I didn't ask how. Some stuff you just don't want to know. But Clouse had a new home, twelve siblings, and Greta. It wasn't going to be easy. For anyone.

I generally recommend against adopting wildcats. Ferals can be very skittish and distrusting of humans. Most people prefer cats that have a capacity for affection. Cats don't generally slobber all over you like dogs, but it is nice to have a companion you can stroke and warm your lap with. Most cats will not greet you at the door in a frenzy like a dog, but most won't run away and hide, either. Clouse did. Most ferals will. The Fairchilds had a lot of work ahead of them.

The Fairchilds were dedicated to domesticating Clouse, but one of their first attempts at civilizing him was a big mistake. Clouse, who was initially confined to a cage, was petrified of the Fairchilds, terrified of Greta, and scared of the twelve other cats. Sid decided that Clouse would benefit from a little petting, so he stuck a glove on a stick and thrust it in the cage to stroke Clouse. This was as bad an idea as the Edsel. It had the opposite effect, scaring the poor little guy to death and driving him to the back of his cage at the very sight of Sid and his pole.

When the call came to me, the Fairchilds had already

realized their aggressive approach to the socialization process was wrong, but they were truly intent on making Clouse a family pet. They needed help.

First on the agenda was to stop the petting attempts with the glove and stick. Instead, we needed a very gradual, tempered approach to making Clouse feel that humans could be trusted. Clouse was to remain in his cage with the door closed, allowing him to feel safe. The Fairchilds were to feed him several times a day in small quantities, reinforcing the fact that their approach to the cage was going to have a positive result. I even suggested that the Fairchilds keep the cat a tad hungry at all times, so he would anticipate their arrival and eventually look forward to the food.

The Fairchilds combined this frequent feeding with soft-spoken words to Clouse and simply sat in the room and quietly read or played a board game while the cat ate. But no petting. Not yet. This was too big a leap for a cat like Clouse. He needed more time to build his confidence.

In about two weeks, there was some notable improvement. Instead of crouching in the back of the cage, Clouse ventured to the front of the enclosure where the Fairchilds were now leaving tiny bits of food. He would still retreat after finding his morsel, but on rare occasions he would rub against the cage door and let the Fairchilds touch him. Not every time, mind you, but these were all small victories.

There was more improvement over the next two weeks. With the cage's front door left open, Clouse ventured around his room—partly in search of food, which the Fairchilds now placed strategically around the area. In some cases, the Fairchilds would make a row of tidbits that led right to them. Sometimes Clouse would rub against Sylvia's leg, but I still cautioned them about petting. Clouse needed to stay in control of the process, warming up at his own pace. That was the only way this could work.

Will integrating a thirteenth cat be successful? Cats are territorial, and every cat develops a slightly different posture toward every other cat. The spectrum of any relationship can range from hostile to indifferent to friendly.

To facilitate this integration, we began by tying Clouse's bedroom door open two inches with a shoelace tied to the doorknob and a nail on the door frame. Clouse became progressively bolder by watching and sometimes interacting with other cats through the aperture in the entrance. Some cats came to see the new guy and seemed to like him. Some came and hissed at him. Some couldn't be bothered. That's the way cats are.

More improvement. The Fairchilds even got in an appreciated stroke now and then, which was fine as long as they didn't push it. The cats who were interested were now allowed to be in the bedroom with Clouse. He still had his cage as a refuge, but more and more he seemed comfortable with the interaction with his fellow felines.

Within six months, the Fairchilds accomplished quite a feat. They took in a feral cat and with patience and dedication managed to assimilate the new pet into their existing pet population. Clouse would probably never be quite as warm, cuddly, and friendly as the other cats, but he had made tremendous progress and was now roaming the house, retreating to his room on occasion for refuge.

Oh, and what about Greta? It's hard to ignore a ninety-pound sheepdog in a story. Greta and Clouse were actually starting to hit it off. In fact, Clouse kind of looked to Greta as his protector, even cuddling up next to her to sleep. Yes, he loved Greta, but he loved Greta's pillow even more, often plopping down on it when Greta was otherwise occupied yapping at the front doorbell or barking at the mailman.

When Greta wasn't around, Clouse owned the pillow. Incredibly, Clouse figured out that if he brushed against the curio cabinet in the dining room and rattled the china, Greta sprang to her feet to investigate. Bingo. Clouse ran to the vacant pillow and went to sleep.

Although Clouse was cat number thirteen, he was a very lucky cat, indeed. Mrs. Fairchild wanted more cats, but Sid finally put his foot down—something you must be very careful doing in a home with thirteen cats.

CAT NIPS

- Don't threaten or challenge a shy, fearful cat; let her build confidence in her surroundings.
- Hand-feeding a cat develops trust and acceptance.
- Let a shy/fearful cat show a need for interaction before you attempt to touch or pet him.
- Dedication, patience, and time are a must to gain a fearful cat's trust and love.

Part Four

Destruction

"Thousands of years ago, cats were worshipped as gods. Cats have never forgotten this."

—Unknown

"As every cat owner knows, nobody owns a cat."

—Ellen Perry Berkeley

Chapter 21

THE VELVETEEN HABIT

"This cat is going to be the death of me," said Mrs. Haberman over the phone.

Well, I had heard that sentiment hundreds of times in my practice. Pets can be troublesome. That's why we wrote this book. But this was one time that you could take the complaints literally.

Mrs. Haberman was on oxygen, and the long tube from her nose was attached to the tank several feet away on the floor, allowing Mrs. Haberman to be mobile in her home while staying connected to her lifeline. Incredibly, her cat Velvet was chewing holes in that tube.

Velvet, like many cats, loved cords of any type. The consistency seems to appeal to cats. Generally, cats are not as prone to chewing problems as dogs, but cats, sometimes out of boredom, do become obsessed with specific objects. Some cats suck on fabrics, almost like a pacifier. Siamese and Burmese cats (and blends of the two) frequently prefer wool, which has some serious medical implications when the material is actually ingested. Other cats like plastic, carpet, and other fabric, string included. I once counseled a caretaker whose cat chewed door jambs, table legs, and windowsills.

Velvet, by the way, even liked piano chords (she didn't know what a homonym was) and would often lay across the strings of the baby grand piano and pluck them. This was not nearly as life threatening as chewing the oxygen cord, but Velvet was tone deaf and couldn't play a lick.

Velvet needed to be stopped quickly. Sometimes behavioral changes must be approached methodically, but this required drastic measures. First, the cat had to be confined when Mrs. H. was sleeping or gone from the house. Velvet was to have her own room with no cords, no temptations, but plenty of cat toys—things to bat around, like balls and milk bottle rings, and other toys hanging on door knobs.

But Velvet could not be secluded all the time; she was, after all, Mrs. Haberman's pet, and her companion. That was the whole point of having the cat. The key now was to make the all the cords and the tubing less interesting to Velvet. First, we determined where the cord actually hit the ground, and we negotiated the tubing so as little as possible was stretched along the floor. Where many cords converged from lamps and other appliances, we stretched the lines through cardboard boxes so they were less visible and accessible.

We wrapped the exposed, accessible oxygen tubes and cords in duct tape, which by itself probably was an attraction, and then as a deterrent added a healthy dose of bitter apple, which adhered nicely to the tape. Bitter apple works best when the pet has been given a strong dose on its lips and mouth so that the very smell of it deters the pet from coming any closer. Another option we had was aluminum foil, which is unpleasant to a cat's teeth when biting, but foil is sometimes tougher to work with since it can slip around and even come off.

Mrs. Haberman was also armed with a water pistol, which she carried in her belt like Annie Oakley, to offer a timely squirt at Velvet when she expressed interest in her oxygen tubes or electric cords.

And Mrs. Haberman also got the opportunity to do a little home cooking. I asked her to take some rawhide dog stick treats (yes, dog treats), soak them in some tuna juice or rub them with anchovy paste, and stick them in the freezer. Because Velvet loved to chew, we were redirecting her habit to a more enticing alternative. We also changed Velvet's food from canned to dry, providing more roughage and another mouthing outlet.

One of the problems in a home like this, where the caretaker is older and restricted in movement, is that the cat has less opportunity to play and interact. Velvet was bored and needed more exercise, and this contributed to the chewing problem. With some additional cat toys, catnip, a laser light, a fishing pole, and a scratching post, Velvet's chewing diminished quickly and soon stopped.

Mrs. Haberman felt safe again in her home. Why not? She could hit a burglar in the eye with a water gun from twenty paces.

CAT NIPS

- Use a piece of cotton to give your cat a good overdose of bitter apple on the lips. Then the very whiff will make it a more effective deterrent.

- Redirect a cat's destructiveness toward an appropriate alternative, and reinforce the appropriate behavior with praise and treats.

- If your cat's a chewer, feed him dry cat food. That's an additional form of exercise and a good redirection of his chomping needs.

Chapter 22

LIVING OUT A SCRATCHING

It was hard to tell what was more in tatters, Hillary Windham's nerves or her brand-new sofa. If I had a dollar for everyone who ever called me about a cat with a penchant for clawing and scratching, I could have replaced Mrs. Windham's sofa—several times over.

Cat owners are well aware of this clawing propensity, a natural behavior that you cannot stop, but one that you can direct and control. The culprit in this case was Roosevelt, a one-year-old tabby that had ruined the old living room sofa and was now eyeing the new one. When Mrs. Windham called, she didn't know where to turn. But whenever she turned, Roosevelt was at the new blue sofa or the matching chair.

Roosevelt never touched the lime green love seat. Why? No one will ever know. But we do know this: Every cat has certain preferences. Some may be identifiable, like favoring certain textures and objects; some cats prefer scratching a vertical surface to a horizontal one. But oftentimes you don't know what turns them on unless you watch what and how they scratch.

Why was Roosevelt scratching? Was he possessed? Yes, possessed of a behavior that pre-dates couches and chairs. At the top of the list was Roosevelt's inborn need to condition his nails and mark his territory. By scratching and clawing, not only did Roosevelt leave visual signs of his personal appearance at that location, but scent glands in his paws left a distinct odor. Think of it as interior decorating with your signature stamp on it.

For Roosevelt, scratching was great exercise. It stretched his whole body, specifically the muscles in the front quarters as well as the tendons in his legs and feet. Roosevelt didn't need any equipment; his body was his portable gym.

Scratching and clawing are stress relievers, the equivalent of a good workout or a vigorous sprint. Quite simply, it was sheer pleasure. Which is why preventing clawing and scratching would be cruel—not that you really could do that. The behavior is going to surface somewhere; you just want to control which surface that turns out to be. In some cases, I've suggested clients move the cat's favorite old couch or chair into a separate room so the cat can claw away to his heart's content.

Many cat owners look for the solution to this problem by heading to the pet store for some kind of scratching post. Remember two things in your quest: First, as mentioned above, every cat has a personal preference for what he likes to scratch, so after you have lugged some hunk of carpet-covered lumber back to your house, Roosevelt or Eisenhower or Jefferson may look at you as if to say, "Why did you even bother?" Now, instead of a scratching post, you have a conversation piece for your cocktail parties. In addition, be very sure that the post is secure and firmly based. Your cat must feel that he can maneuver safely without the post giving or swaying.

For all these reasons, I recommend that you build your own scratching post. You may have already detected some of your cat's preferences. Where possible, buy an extra piece of fabric to match the new furniture or, if you've decided to chuck the couch that has been destroyed, save a pillow or some fabric.

Then take a four-by-four, at least three feet long, and secure it to a two-foot by two-foot square, one-inch-thick base. Wrap the post with a carpet remnant, backside out, then cover the carpet with the fabric of choice and rub fresh catnip into the material periodically. You now have your post. You don't have to drag some ugly contraption home from the store; you have made your own ugly contraption.

Because cats are creatures of habit, it is generally best to place the post near the original sight of destruction. There you can reward appropriate scratching with treats, a scratch of your own under the feline's chin or the side of his face, or initiation of play with interactive toys. Cat toys should also be available at the site as a possible distraction. Just make sure all associations with the cat post are positive.

In addition, you need to dissuade your cat from the inappropriate scratching. Vinyl slip covers, aluminum foil, or double-sided tape can be effective to cover areas where the cat has previously done her handiwork.

If your cat scratches on horizontal surfaces, like carpets, throw an extra carpet remnant over the location where he is clawing. That often serves his needs and saves you time and money.

Another very effective technique is the use of balloons. Most cats (dogs, too) are skittish when it comes to the popping sound of a balloon. Once you show your cat a few times what a busted balloon sounds like, you can then hang a few inflated ones from a thread on or near the furniture you are trying to protect.

There are a few other options. I won't get into the declawing debate, which raises a lot of hackles, but cat nails certainly can be trimmed. It's really very simple—about as simple as giving a cat a bath, so good luck. There are also commercial coverings for the cat's claws that will allow the cat to scratch but render him less destructive.

To restate the obvious, you need to refocus your cat's attention and give him an appropriate outlet with reinforcement for this basic instinct. Let your cat know that if he wants to live in your house, he has to abide by a new set of rules.

That, Roosevelt, is what we call the new deal.

CAT NIPS

- Observe your cat carefully to determine her scratching preferences. That will help you find alternatives she will like.
- Reward appropriate scratching. Prevent inappropriate scratching.
- Whether you build it or buy it, a scratching post must be sturdy.
- Save your new couch by saving the old one. Stick it in the basement for your cat's scratching pleasure.

Part Five

Other Misbehaviors

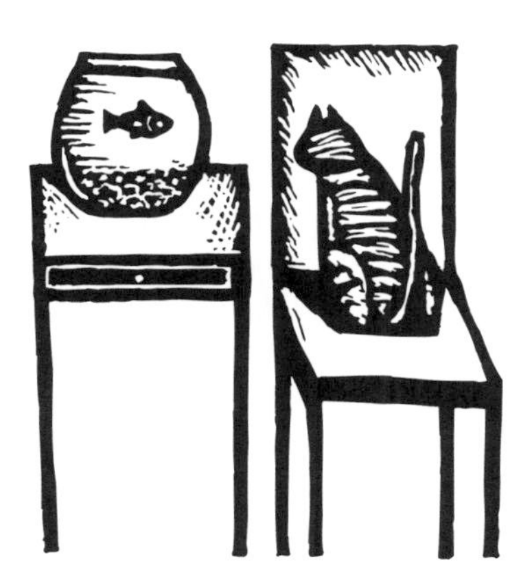

"To assume a cat's asleep is a grave mistake. He can close his eyes and keep both his ears awake."

—Aileen Fisher

"Cats are connoisseurs of comfort."

—James Herriot

Chapter 23

STAR SEARCH

Here's the dilemma I was confronted with when I received a distressed phone call from a couple very much in love. They were having relationship problems. It wasn't that they were fighting like cats and dogs. It was their cats and dog that were fighting like cats and dogs.

Lois loved her cats. Jim loved his dog. Lois loved Jim. Jim loved Lois. There was no more love to go around.

Here were the culprits in this feud: two black cats named Sirius and Vega, a three-legged cat named Rigel, and a dog named Tippy. Tippy was a Scottie, a breed of dog that traditionally has little tolerance for rodents or cats. I'd be tempted to say that many Scotties are cat haters, but that would be unkind. It would not, however, be untrue.

Jim and Lois wanted to make a perfect blended family, but their approach was somewhat analogous to putting olive oil and water in a blender. Bursts of activity, a lot of noise, but a waste of time. When Jim brought Tippy to Lois's house, there was total chaos. The cats freaked out. One hid behind the dryer, one hid in the pantry, one jumped on top of the counter, one hid under the bed, one hid in the basement, and one hid under the couch.

Wait a second, that's too many cats. Well, it seemed like there were cats hiding everywhere.

If the cats were taken to Tippy's house, they panicked even more. Not familiar with the terrain, they didn't know where to hide. Tippy got very protective of his turf. It was like a search-and-destroy mission. Remember how cartoonists draw cats that are scared, with all four limbs extended in mid-air, hair standing straight up? That's it. You've got the picture.

Jim and Lois had already delayed their marriage for more than a year. I explained to them that this hostility between dog and cat was certainly not a new problem. True, many felines and canines live happily together, but there exists a predisposition to mistrust each other. This mistrust only goes back ten thousand years in history, so I figured I could wrap this baby up with a couple of phone calls. Yeah, right.

The first issue was where the newlyweds should live after the marriage. Believe it or not, this was an important decision to make regarding the animals. In either case, there was bound to be unrest, but I determined that the cats would be more comfortable in their own home. Dogs are instinctively guardians of their territory, so we didn't want to give Tippy home field advantage.

It's always difficult to tell clients that part of the problem lies with them. Actually, most of the problem lies with them, but I have to be a diplomat. In this case, Jim needed to exercise a bit more control over the dog. We began by placing Tippy on a lead. But even if his movements were restricted, his barking scared the bejeebers out of the feline triumvirate. To squelch the yapping, we used a squirt from a water gun in Tippy's face, preceded by the command "quiet!" This doesn't hurt, of course, but it's a nice dose of reality and I think a touch humiliating, as well. He soon stopped barking when he heard the command and saw the water bottle. This was a big step toward the cats' peace of mind. Was a quieter dog a gentler dog? Could be. It seemed like a good start. And Tippy enjoyed tasty rewards for just watching the cats and not harassing them.

The cats seemed to gain confidence when Tippy was tied and quiet and didn't have freedom to patrol the house. The cats grew bolder, peering around couches and observing Tippy from the top of the fridge. We also gave the cats their own room, protected by a baby gate, allowing the cats an impenetrable refuge. Cats could go in and out under the gate. The Scottie couldn't.

The dog was slowly becoming more of a curiosity than a threat. BIG difference. You could almost hear Rigel saying to Sirrus and Vega, "So what are you guys doing tonight? Wanna go watch the dog? Let's get better seats than yesterday."

I had a few other ideas. I wanted the cats and dog to be comfortable with each other's scents, so I had Jim and Lois wipe their animals down and exchange the malodorous towels. Remember, animals are scent driven. In this case, familiarity bred content.

During the day, when Jim and Lois were at work, Jim brought Tippy to Lois's house and put him in his crate, allowing the cats to fully enjoy their space but further reinforcing that the dog was not a menace. When Jim and Lois were home together, the dog was always on the lead, usually tied to something, increasingly gaining more and more freedom, but dragging his cord and getting treats for his appropriate behavior.

Jim and Lois began to think that a blended family could be a reality. Perfect harmony was still a few months away, but progress was significant enough that they booked the caterer.

One day after the wedding, I got a call. It was Lois.

"Dr. Sampson, we all slept together last night. Even the three-legged cat jumped up on the bed. None of them were afraid."

For the first time in the age of Aquarius, all the stars were aligned.

CAT NIPS

- The less your dog terrorizes your cat, the quicker the cat will gain confidence. Separate or monitor them carefully.
- Cats need to know there is a safe haven, a place to go where the dog can't.
- If the pets in your house are not getting along, separate them, but let them see each other through partially open doors. Familiarity impedes contempt.

Chapter 24

GETTING A LITTLE R&R

This is the story of two cats, Robby and Regina, who lived peacefully together. There was little to interrupt their idyllic lives, which consisted primarily of lounging, purring, and preening. Such is the typical existence of most homebound felines.

But that was to all to change when who should appear on the scene? GOLDIE.

We will use all capital letters for GOLDIE's name because we want to remind you throughout the story that this was not a typical cat. GOLDIE had more energy than she knew what to do with.

When the Goldbergs found GOLDIE, they assumed they could just add her to the feline mix without a worry in the world. Often, this is the case. However, cats can sometimes have a problem integrating because of territorial or hierarchy issues.

When GOLDIE entered the picture, the picture got very blurry. Blurry because GOLDIE cavorted through the house like Spider-Man on speed. GOLDIE wanted to play. She had so much energy that she terrorized Robby and Regina who were not looking for any additional extracurricular activity. They enjoyed being regular old cats. They liked that lounging, purring, preening thing.

But GOLDIE liked the thrill of the chase and she spent a good part of the day running Robby and Regina ragged. There was no R&R for R&R. When the chases started resulting in fights, the phone call came to me.

"My cats are fighting like cats and dogs," said Mrs. Goldberg. Which is an odd way to put it, but I got the point.

The first thing we had to do was create a situation where the original two cats could interact with GOLDIE without the possibility of a hot pursuit. As I've done in many other instances discussed in this book, I asked Mrs. Goldberg to create a cat room for R&R with the door tied with a shoelace and nail leaving a two-inch gap. This allowed the cats to see each other and even play pawsies, but not fully interact or fight. We also rotated the cats so they did not feel as though they "owned" the space. Remember, it was important they not be separated completely, because that would have only increased the mystique and motivated GOLDIE even more when they did cross paths.

In addition, I had the Goldbergs take a pair of cloth gloves and stroke GOLDIE with one glove and the other two cats with the another glove. Then the Goldbergs essentially swapped the scents so that GOLDIE smelled like R&R, and R&R were covered in GOLDIE's odors. We also fed the cats near the opening of the door at the same time, making suppertime a family affair, whether they liked it or not.

They later installed a screen door on the bedroom to separate R&R from GOLDIE, expanding to full visual contact. Here, too, we kept the door tied ajar so they could physically interact. We wanted their future interactions to be ho-hum. Kind of like, "Oh, it's you again."

Progress, I admit, was slow, and any full interaction often resulted in a chase of epic proportions. I suggested conditioning GOLDIE to a harness and a six-foot tether so that the Goldbergs could exercise control over her at all times. When R&R ventured out into the open living room, GOLDIE would attempt to lurch but was quickly hampered by the tether. We also distracted GOLDIE with a fishing pole with an interactive toy to redirect her energy. And when that failed we added a little spritz of water in GOLDIE's face to further dampen her spirit.

We were moderately successful, but there was something about GOLDIE that resisted the behavior modification. The prospect of real improvement was being slowed by GOLDIE's persistence in lurching, constantly undoing any progress we had made. This was one of those times when I opted to help the process along with a little antianxiety medication for GOLDIE.

During this time, I encouraged the Goldbergs to feed the cats together with GOLDIE on a tether, reinforcing a period of time when they would all be near each other without the threat of a GOLDIE chase. Even GOLDIE preferred eating over chasing.

After a few months, GOLDIE was slowly weaned off the medication, and I asked the Goldbergs to make a concerted effort to keep her well exercised. I often say, "A tired cat is a snoozing cat." In addition, we were sure to always reward GOLDIE with a treat just for being, well, a cat, and for ignoring R&R in her presence.

And so we reach the end of the story. I had not heard from the Goldbergs in several months. Then came the phone call.

"Well, we adopted another cat. We couldn't resist him. I'm afraid he's just like GOLDIE. He's chasing the other three cats. What should we do, Dr. Sampson?"

"Okay," I said, getting out my notes. "This is going to sound very familiar."

CAT NIPS

- Use a screen door as the door for the cat room to socialize cats with each other.

- Use a cloth to rub one cat and then rub the other cat to transfer the odor. It greases the wheels of friendship when you smell like your enemy.

- When separating cats, prevent them from becoming territorial by alternating the rooms where they are kept.

Chapter 25

FAT CAT

You don't have to be a Hoosier veterinarian to recognize a fat cat. Seeing the Garfield image everywhere gives you a pretty good visual image of a portly feline.

Bubba was Garfield's understudy. Although I don't specifically recall the Browns feeding him lasagna, I doubt Bubba would have rejected it. Finicky was not a word you associated with Bubba.

Dining for this pet was an all-consuming activity, and Bubba consumed pretty much everything. He yowled at meal time; he yowled when it wasn't mealtime. That's twenty-four-hour yowling.

The Browns were pretty much pushovers. They would push over the side of the table any leftovers they had onto Bubba's dish. The Browns figured if they just fed him, he would quiet down. These are the kind of people who really need this book.

Whenever Bubba threw a little food fit, he got fed. If he jumped on Mr. B.'s lap and rolled his chubby little eyes (yes, even his eyes were chubby), Mr. B. fed him. At four o'clock in the morning when Bubba wanted a snack, Mrs. B got up and fed him. Then Bubba wanted a snack at six in the morning. Up again.

Bubba ate and ate, usually so much and so fast that he would throw up. It reached the point where Bubba didn't want to go to sleep because he might miss a snack. He had both a medical and a behavioral problem. When the Browns called me, they needed advice. And a good night's sleep.

Ironically, Mr. Brown owned a restaurant. He knew that if the customer was happy with the food, he'd keep coming back. So when I explained that the family was just reinforcing Bubba's food mania by feeding him as soon he walked into the restaurant (the kitchen), I knew Mr. Brown would understand.

The first thing we did was eliminate the standard meal time. Bubba would no longer be fed in a bowl at a specific hour. Instead, the day's allotment of dry *diet* food would be scattered around the house on plates in tiny quantities over a sixteen-hour period. By also spreading the food out on the plate, it would be tougher for Bubba to gorge his food, which had contributed to the vomiting problem. Now there was kibble under the couch, behind the umbrella stand, next to the stereo. Kibble everywhere. He only had to be shown once where there was food, and Bubba would find it.

It was important that the routine and times were staggered. They did not want Bubba to whine. In fact, if he did, that was a signal *not* to give him food.

If Bubba wanted something to eat, he had to hunt for his snack. This had a dual effect. It stopped Bubba from hounding (excuse the expression, cat lovers) the Browns, and at the same time it gave Bubba a little exercise. Instead of just waiting for food, Bubba had to search out his next morsel, just like the old days, millions of years ago.

As noted, Bubba was never to be fed following meowing, yowling, pawing, or eye rolling. In fact, if Bubba reverted to this annoying approach, he was to be ignored. And if he persisted, he was marched (it looked more like a waddle) into the bathroom for a little time-out. At night, the laundry room served as his bedroom. We did not want Bubba scavenging for food at night. People sleep at night. So should cats. If Bubba was unhappy or hungry, his cries would go both unheard and unheeded. In the morning, his exit from his "room" was rewarded by allowing him to scavenge for food in one of the many places food had been placed. I did not want Bubba to see the room as a punishment—just a resting place where food was not available.

This is all a little trickier than it sounds. Food was the problem here, yet food is often the best way to reward a pet and reinforce appropriate behavior. In this case, the issue was where, when, and how the food would be dispensed. Bubba was starting to get the message: Eating was okay; being compulsive was not. And Bubba discovered that you have to earn your right to eat.

And, to introduce an exercise program into Bubba's routine, the Browns played with the cat with interactive toys and laser lights multiple times a day.

In time, the Browns were slowly able to let Bubba use his bowl again, dividing his allotment of food three times throughout the day, but I encouraged the Browns to still hide small amounts of food occasionally to keep Bubba on his toes. The more he was on his toes and the less he was on back sleeping on the couch, the better chance we had of reducing his weight.

Bubba slimmed down, and the Browns were now in control of his diet. Oh, Bubba still loved to eat, but

Garfield's reputation as the fattest cat in town was no longer in jeopardy.

CAT NIPS

- If your cat is fat and is motivated by food, hide her regular food and treats to make her work for them.
- If you're not sure what your cat is thinking, it's probably this: "What's in it for me?"
- Sometimes when you think you're modifying your cat's behavior, he's modifying yours.

Chapter 26

PARTY ANIMAL

Over the years, I have been called as an expert witness in legal cases involving incidents where someone was injured by another person's pet and then looked to put the bite on the pet owner—financially.

I have worked with plaintiff and defendant; however, most of the time I am on the side of the animal and the owner. My role is to explain why the animal behaved in that manner and to establish whether the pet was (or was not) vicious or whether the attack may have been provoked. Such testimony helps establish appropriate damages. Since insurance companies are usually represented by both sides, hefty awards loom as a possibility. I've seen them go as high as $250,000.

I also assist in jury selection, hoping to find pet owners, who usually are more understanding of an animal's needs and instincts. And women are usually better jurors for the defense, often being even more sensitive to the animal's issues involved. I have also assisted the lawyers in developing questions for depositions, which elicit information that will be helpful to the jury. In many instances, the cases never reach trial.

Most cases involve an animal bite. Cat bite cases are

relatively rare, but when the bites occur they can cause serious injuries. Cat bites are similar to inoculations. The pin-like teeth can imbed the bacteria from the cat's mouth through the skin, deep into the muscle and often hitting bone. Dog bites appear more dangerous on the surface—literally—but in reality the bites may be only torn flesh, and the resulting bleeding may actually flush out the bacteria. All animal bites must be taken seriously, but do not underestimate the risks of a cat bite.

And that was exactly what happened in one case where I was called to testify. Purgatory, a pale gray neutered male, enjoyed roaming the neighborhood. He had his route where neighbors would often reward him with leftovers, petting, and attention. Oh, he had a home—a very nice home—but eating out was one of his favorite pastimes.

That brought Purgatory to the Gablingers' home the night of Mr. Gablinger's fiftieth birthday party. Not the least bit shy, Purgatory slithered in through the porch door, no doubt attracted to the aroma of the shrimp dip.

Purgatory wove in and out of legs and was pretty much ignored by the group. But at one point, people tired of passing the cocktail franks around, so they snatched Purgatory off the floor and began passing him around. Purgatory was very good natured, but, as I later testified, there is only so much even a friendly cat can handle. By the time Purgatory reached the arms of Mrs. Kendelwood, he had been fondled enough. Mrs. Kendelwood let out a scream as Purgatory's tiny teeth sunk deep into her wrist. In a flash, Purgatory was out the porch door.

The bite smarted, but the tiny wounds did not look very menacing, so Mrs. Kendelwood did little more than wash her wrist and head back to the hors d'oeuvre table.

Within a few days, Mrs. Kendelwood's arm began to swell and stiffen. She was admitted to the hospital and treated with IV antibiotics for five days. She was in pretty severe pain and missed a few weeks of work due to pain and stiffness in her wrist. It was a lawsuit waiting to happen. And so it did.

Here was a case where I was hired by the defendant. My role was to help the jury understand that the cat, which had never displayed any inappropriate aggression before, had been so overstimulated by the manhandling that its bite response had been provoked (which was entirely understandable). I directed my comments to specific members of the jury, recognizing that those with pets deserved a little more eye contact from me. Again, I knew who had pets because I had helped select the jury.

Physicans involved in the case also made it clear that most of Mrs. Kendelwood's medical problems could have been avoided had she been more vigilant and taken appropriate care of the wound.

The trial lasted a few days. Because both sides had stipulated that Purgatory had, indeed, bitten Mrs. Kendelwood, the plaintiff's attorney simply made a case for financial damages suffered by his client and the additional compensation he felt the pain and suffering were worth. During cross-examination, my credibility was challenged as attorneys probed my background and experience with cat behavior, giving me an opportunity to discuss my practice and similar cases. Being a veterinarian for twenty-five years didn't hurt.

The jury came back quickly and, even to my surprise, Mrs. Kendelwood was not awarded a dime. The jury felt that Purgatory and been put through the ringer and that if Mrs. Kendelwood had taken the time to seek immediate medical attention for the bite, the medical issue would not have escalated.

A final note: In some cases, I might be asked by the court to give the animal a temperament evaluation, which would give stronger evidence of the cat's demeanor, demonstrating to the jury or judge that the bite was either atypical or expected behavior for that animal, the result being one of natural or provoked aggression.

By this time, however (the incident was two years old), Purgatory had passed away. Even with a name like Purgatory, we hope he got to a better place. In my opinion and the jury's, he should have.

CAT NIPS

- An overstimulated cat is a potential biter and scratcher.
- In most legal actions, everyone agrees the animal caused injury. The legal question is: What were the circumstances? Was the animal provoked? Could the owners have prevented this?
- Because all cat behavior has a purpose, you can say all behavior is normal. The question is: What is acceptable to you?

Chapter 27

A STROKE OF JEANNIE

This is a very sad story, but only in the beginning. It has a very happy ending, so stick with me. It's also kind of a mystery. See if you can figure it out as we go along.

When Mrs. Butterworth called, she was very upset. You would have been, too. Mrs. Butterworth couldn't have put it more clearly:

"Jeannie doesn't love me anymore."

I try not to jump too far ahead of a client's story, but this is one I could see coming. Over the years, I have gotten literally hundreds of calls like this.

Yes, Mrs. Butterworth was distraught. This was the cat she had raised from the time it was a kitten, the cat she fed every day, the cat whose boxes she cleaned, and the cat she groomed lovingly. Yes, the very the cat that slept next to her at night had slowly over the past year become more and more distant.

In the evening when the Butterworths sat in front of the TV, Jeannie curled up in a ball—six feet away from Mrs. Butterworth. If Mrs. B. tried to hold, caress, or pet Jeannie, the cat was unreceptive, became almost agitated, and bit at Mrs. B.'s hand. Bottom line: Excessive handling and petting triggered the cat to respond with:

"I'm out of here."

Mrs. B was thin-skinned. The result was a bleeding hand and hurt feelings.

Then, to make matters worse (much worse), the cat would jump off her lap, run to Mr. B., and crawl up into his lap. This was the last straw for Mrs. B. "My husband doesn't even like cats," she told me. "He pays no attention to her. In fact, he won't even touch her. She just spends the night in his lap while he reads, watches TV, and falls off to sleep."

Bingo! It was as I had suspected—a case like all the others.

But have you solved the mystery?

Here's a clue: Despite Jeannie's apparent disregard for Mrs. B., the cat did sleep right next to her at night.

Here's another clue: Have you ever noticed that when a cat walks into a room where several people are seated, some cats will often gravitate to the person who is not a cat person? Yes, in a room of cat lovers, it's often the one person who is fearful or not comfortable with cats who finds kitty in her lap or rubbing against her leg. Go figure, huh?

Cats, as you cat people know, are basically independent. Of course, many cats are social with their human companions, but the feline's basic personality is more solitary. As a result, some cats are not predisposed to seek attention. That's why the person who is anxious or even fearful of cats finds an uninvited new friend at that cocktail party. He was the least likely to make a fuss, vocalize his affection for the Siamese, or put out his hand. So the cat goes to *him.*

Jeannie was one of those cats. She had a very low

tolerance for stimulation. Mrs. B. was a hugger, a caresser, and a petter. And the more Jeannie tried to distance herself from the attention, the more lovey-dovey Mrs. B. got. That's called a vicious cycle.

Cats do want some affection, but most of them want it on their own terms. They are controllers. Dogs, for the most part, put a belly scratch in the same category as a hunk of sirloin. Not so with cats. In fact, prolonged body petting overstimulates many cats and may elicit a bite. Imagine a nonstop tickle.

Mrs. Butterworth needed to limit her affection or, more accurately, change her style. Instead of stroking Jeannie's body with her hand, I suggested that Mrs. B. restrict her contact with Jeannie to one or two fingers, and that she limit the touching to the cat's head and facial area. The cat's head has tiny scent glands that are used for marking. That's why cats often run their heads against your leg. They are saying: You are my person. Touching those areas gently is an appreciated form of stimulation and self-marking for most cats. Jeannie liked it. Mrs. B. was doing the marking for her.

But we also had some conditioning to do. True, I wanted to teach Mrs. B. how to effectively stroke Jeannie, but we also wanted Jeannie to learn the value of Mrs. B.'s affection. Mrs. B. carried treats in her pockets, and whenever Jeannie did venture into her lap, she was rewarded while being petted intermittently on the head and face with one finger.

I also asked Mrs. B. to be stingy with her affection. Instinctively, an animal that is getting just a little affection will probably yearn for a bit more. This is true of humans, too, but I'm only licensed to help dogs and cats.

Slowly but surely, Jeannie started warming up to Mrs. B. She sat closer to her mistress, tolerated a bit more stroking, without biting her and remained her nightly sleeping companion.

And, of course, Mr. Butterworth was happy, as well. His lap was now free for a beer and a slice of pizza.

CAT NIPS

- A cat views moving objects as prey, so don't use hands and feet to play with your cat. Interact with toys, instead. Your hands will appreciate this when you try to pet your cat.

- Pet your cat based on his affection appetite. Not yours.

Chapter 28

SAM THE SHAM

I bet you are wondering how my own pets behave. You are probably thinking that all my animals are perfectly disciplined.

Oh, you weren't thinking that? Well, someone has a big mouth, then.

Our first three years with Sam the cat were pretty uneventful—no problems that would have prompted me to call someone like *me* on the phone.

True, Sam was needy: laps and loving 8/7 (That's like 24/7, but cats sleep at least 16 hours a day). Sam demanded constant attention with a crabby cry. When my wife, Elaine, was doing the crossword puzzle, there was Sam on her lap, four feet across, one head down. Elaine, like many pet owners, responded to the cat's wiles and thus created a controlling feline who became cranky if he didn't get his way—and who knew how to get exactly what he wanted. He was a high-maintenance cat.

When Liesel, a schnauzer puppy, entered the family, it seemed like we might get a reprieve from the clinginess. The cat and dog bonded immediately, and their antics together were a source of great amusement to Elaine and me. A favorite activity of Liesel as she grew was to grab

Sam by the head and neck and drag him along the slippery kitchen floor. Sam loved it and spent most of his life full of Liesel's slobber. They were soul mates. As you'll see, maybe they should have been inmates.

As Liesel was being housebroken, she discovered that when she returned to the front door (with Sam right behind her), Elaine provided them both with a treat. The treat-giving was supposed to be a reward for Liesel's adherence to traditional housebreaking requirements, but animals cannot make that association. To them, the reward is for coming to the front door—not for proper potty procedure.

I hate to admit this, but the dog and cat soon conditioned both of *us*. I knew we were being manipulated, my wife knew we were being manipulated, and the dynamic duo knew we were being manipulated. It reached a point where Sam would cry to go out the back door many times a day, then show up at the front door sixty seconds later. Liesel would be in tow, both running to the pantry door to beg for treats. Not that they deserved it. They hadn't done their business, unless their business was fooling Elaine and me.

In the spring, when daylight came earlier, it was not uncommon for Sam to cry at the door around 4:30 in the morning. My wife would get up and let the little schemer outside. He would come back a few minutes later and get a treat. Elaine would go back to bed. In twelve-step programs I think they call this enabling.

Finally, we agreed enough's enough. "Sam has a litter box. Let's have him use it." Because Elaine was already on the edge with this cat, she didn't want to interrupt the delicate balance between the cat's demands and her own sanity. She wanted to leave bad enough alone. The tension between my wife and the crabby, demanding cat gave Elaine TMJ, which I can't prove, but we know this: When the cat died, the disorder cleared up.

It was time to put my experience to good use. Finally.

So whenever the cranky cry from Sam was heard at the door in the middle of the night, I went and quickly picked him up and deposited him in the garage. I'm not one who sees human qualities in dogs and cats, but you should have seen the expression on Sam's face. After a few mornings with that approach, Sam got the picture, and his early morning requests to exit the house stopped.

And to further strengthen this reconditioning, Elaine and I accompanied Liesel when she went out during the day so that she could be rewarded at the appropriate time, not when she returned to the front door.

At some point in all of this, we changed Sam's name to Grabis, a more fitting label, we thought, for a crabby, cranky cat that had managed, at least for a while, to live in a house with a supposed expert in pet behavior and his wife, and still twist them around his little paw.

You have to admit that I am very honest to openly acknowledge this. You also have to admit I was very smart to make this the last chapter.

CAT NIPS

- A good way to let your cat know you are unhappy with his behavior is fifteen minutes in a time-out room.

ABOUT THE AUTHORS

Gary Sampson and Dick Wolfsie with his cat, Benson.

Gary R. Sampson, DVM, is a native of Minnesota and a 1960 graduate of the University of Minnesota Veterinary School. He opened a private veterinary clinic while also serving as the Director of Mayo Research Animal Care Facilities at the University of Minnesota's School of Medicine. He moved to Indianapolis in the '60s and spent thirty-one years in animal products research management at Eli Lilly and Co. He also has authored numerous scientific publications. Dr. Sampson has devoted the last twenty years to helping beleaguered pet owners with their problem dogs and cats, although his work is mostly correcting the owners' behaviors.

Dr. Sampson lives in Indianapolis with his wife, Elaine, and Lizzie, their standard poodle. He has two children and three grandchildren who, unlike some of his patients, are all perfectly behaved.

Dick Wolfsie has worked in television and radio for more than twenty-five years and is currently a features reporter for WISH-TV in Indianapolis. An Emmy Award winner, he is the author of seven books, including *Barney: The Stray Beagle Who Became a TV Star and Stole Our Hearts*. Dick's weekly humor column is syndicated in twenty-five newspapers in central Indiana. He lives in Indianapolis with his wife, Mary Ellen, his son, Brett, Toby the beagle, and Benson the cat.

Books of Interest

Also in the Pet Peeves series:

Dog Dilemmas: Simple Solutions to Everyday Problems

By Gary R. Sampson, DVM with Dick Wolfsie

Meet Apache, an Irish setter who was petrified of birds. Whiskers, a Border collie who herded cats. And Noah, a toy poodle who took a bite out of the Maytag repairman's backside. Discover how veterinarian Gary Sampson solved these and other problems of great pup-portions—and learn to resolve your own dog's behavior issues at the same time.

Each chapter in *Dog Dilemmas* contains a practical lesson you can apply to your own relationship with your dog. These stories will have you laughing along and, more important, will leave you a bit wiser when it comes to establishing appropriate behavior in your best friend.

Paperback Price $9.99
ISBN: 1-57860-226-2

Barney
The Stray Beagle Who Became a TV Star and Stole Our Hearts

By Dick Wolfsie

The greatest Barney moments, told by his faithful human sidekick—a book destined to make dog lovers laugh, cry, and howl at the moon.

When TV Reporter Dick Wolfsie took in the tiny stray beagle shivering on his front step, he had no idea that the dog would become more than just a faithful companion. Barney the Beagle's career in the public eye included three thousand shows, fourteen commercials, and twelve straight years on the air.

If you followed Barney's antics over the years, you'll recognize your favorite Barney stories here, plus more than a few surprises. If you missed Barney on TV, here's your chance to meet an unforgettable beagle who had heart, brains, and moxie to spare.

Paperback Price $14.99
ISBN: 1-57860-167-3